BARTENDING INSIDE-OUT

The Guide to Profession, Profit, and Fun

Lori Marcus

Cadillac Press

BARTENDING INSIDE-OUT
The Guide to Profession Profit and Fun

Published by: Cadillac Press

LM@bio4u.us

Produced and printed in the United States of America
Third edition
Copyright © 1997, 2003, 2008 by Lori Marcus

Library of Congress Catalog Card Number: 96-85958

ISBN: 9780964201972

Cover design, book layout
and beer graphics by:
RileyWorks.com

BARTENDING
INSIDE-OUT

Acknowledgments

Many thanks to all of the friends and fellow bartenders whose contributions made this book possible, and to Libby Glassware for providing images of glassware. Special thanks to Shawn R. from The San Francisco School of Bartending for editorial input.

Warning/Disclaimer

Every attempt has been made to provide accurate information in regard to the subject matter covered. This book is sold with the understanding that neither the author nor publisher are qualified to render legal, tax, or other professional advice. If legal or other expert assistance is required, seek the services of a professional. The opinions and suggestions given in this book offer service options and are not intended to supersede existing bar policies.

Contents

INTRODUCTION
TO THE WORLD OF
BARTENDING

Perhaps one of the most annoying and fre-
quently asked questions of a bartender is —
"Why aren't you smiling?"
Invariably this is asked while your bar is five
deep with customers, you're out of beer,
out of glasses, out of ice, and out of your mind!
You ponder this question as you pour his draft
beer (…should I answer truthfully?).
Suddenly, the keg blows, spewing beer suds all
over your questioning customer.
The corners of your mouth begin an
upward curve,
– Your smile returns – You find your rhythm –
" Who's next? - Two Golden Cadillacs? -
No problem! "

**WELCOME TO THE HOSPITALITY
BUSINESS !!**

THE ROLE OF A BARTENDER

Location and decor will bring customers into a bar for the first time. It is the role of the service personnel to make sure that these customers come back again and again.

A bartender is an entertainer: the lead act, stage manager, and director of the show. It is up to him or her to create a friendly atmosphere by interpreting each customer's mood, attitude, and needs. A successful bartender knows just how much (or how little) entertainment to provide.

A bartender must possess a good sense of humor, be diplomatic, have a good attitude and appearance, and be a team player.

Good hand-eye coordination and a keen sense of peripheral vision are necessities.

Knowing what comes next, thinking ahead, and making each move count are essential.

Each bartender develops his own style. It is important to match your style and personality to a bar that allows you to be yourself and enjoy yourself.

BARTENDING BURN OUT

A bartender is hard at work when the rest of the country is on vacation, has the weekend off or a big night out. Most times, the bartending profession will offer you an enjoyable job that allows you to be the host of a party each time you work. Other times, bartending can bring out the worst in the best of us.

Job pressures and the bar environment may encourage one to "join the party." You cannot handle cash, handle liability, or make judgment calls when you party alongside your customers. Discipline yourself, keep healthy, get enough sleep and stay sober.

Eight hours behind the bar is not the same as eight hours at any other job. Keep a schedule that you can handle.

LEARNING TO BARTEND

The best way to learn how to bartend is through "hands-on" experience. Unfortunately, finding a bar that is willing to train you can be hard. If you are presently working in a restaurant/bar as a waiter or bar-back, you are in the optimal position to begin your learning process. Look, listen, ask questions and learn all that you can about specific drinks, garnishes, and liqueurs.

There are also many bartending schools out there that can provide you with basic skills, knowledge, and job placement. Ask around and find one with a good solid reputation.

TOOLS FOR LEARNING

You will need the following tools to help you learn the mechanics of bartending —

EMPTY LIQUOR BOTTLES: Use a generic-shaped liquor bottle with a long neck in order to learn proper handling techniques.

POUR SPOUTS: Make sure that these are not the wide mouth "speed pourers." These fast pour spouts are good for juices and thick liqueurs but make pouring a controlled shot difficult.

SHAKER GLASS and STRAINER: Use the large size, available at most liquor or restaurant supply stores. (see page 113)

SHOT GLASS: Find a two-ounce, lined shot glass. Shot glasses come in different shapes and sizes; you will be learning how to pour a controlled one-ounce shot. (see

GLASSWARE: It is best to use traditional highball, rocks and cocktail glasses. (see page 61)

POURING PROCEDURES

Learning the proper pouring techniques and developing good hand-eye coordination are the only ways to ensure that all drinks are poured accurately and consistently.

There are two types of pouring procedures — measured and free-pouring.

MEASURED POURING

Owners and managers use the measured pouring method in order to keep a bartender from over-pouring alcohol. When a bar requires the use of a shot glass to pour alcohol, they may save on pouring costs (P.C.), but they will lose on time required to pour those drinks, as measured pouring takes twice the time as free-pouring. Most customers prefer watching a bartender free-pour their drink, regardless of how much they pour.

Measured Pouring can be achieved in several ways —

- Liquor guns; similar to a soda gun that are designed to pour a pre-programmed portion only.
- Controlled pour spouts that dispense one shot at a time.
- The required use of a shot glass for pouring.

LEARNING MEASURED POURING

To pour a drink using a measured shot glass or jigger —

- Hold the shot glass over your iced glass.
- Fill the shot glass until it reaches your required pour.
- Empty the measured shot into the glass.
- Rinse out the shot glass. Place it upside down on the bar mat to drain.

It is a good idea to keep two shot glasses for pouring. One for clear liquors and another for colored or cream liquors. Even when you rinse a glass with water, certain oils and flavors can remain behind.

FREE POURING

A professional bartender should be able to free-pour a shot consistently, without measuring or counting. Eventually, you will be able to measure your pour by feel and by knowing where a shot measures up to in your glassware.

The easiest way to learn how to free-pour accurately is to count while you pour. You will find that your count will vary when using different size pour spouts and when pouring thicker liquors.

Each bar has policies regarding the amount of alcohol poured per drink. Some pour one ounce only. Others pour an ounce and a quarter, or ounce and a half. With continuous changes in the laws regarding liability and legal intoxication levels, some bars are cutting back on the amount they pour and some customers are requesting less alcohol and more mix. Next, you will learn to pour a one-ounce shot. After mastering the one-ounce shot, you will be able to adapt for each different pouring situation.

LEARNING TO FREE POUR

Prepare your tools for learning —
Fill two empty liquor bottles with water and top them with pour spouts.

Place a one-ounce shot glass and a rocks glass on a table or countertop that is at least waist high. Be sure to give yourself plenty of room.

When pouring drinks at a bar, always make them on a bar mat. This is a rubber mat placed on the bar, above your ice bin and speed rack, designed to collect any liquid spillage.

Grab the bottle high up around the neck. Always drape your index finger over the base of the pour spout. This prevents the spout from falling out while you pour.

Using your wrist, invert the bottle (almost upside down), over the shot glass. Count the amount of beats it takes to fill the shot glass. Finish your pour by quickly righting the bottle using a twist of your wrist to minimize/prevent spillage.

Improper method

Proper method

Pour the filled shot into a rocks glass; note the level to which it fills the glass. Practice this a few times to establish what count is needed for you to pour a one-ounce shot.

When you feel comfortable with your bottle handling and think you have your count down, reverse your pouring order.

Pour a shot as you have been doing, only this time pour directly into the rocks glass (without ice). Test your accuracy by pouring the contents of the rocks glass back into the shot glass.

Practice and adjust your count until you are able to repeat free- pouring a full shot, give or take a few drops, on a regular basis.

Now, change hands and practice again.

Remember! The liquor bottle must be held by the neck, inverted over the glass (almost upside down) and poured using the wrist. This method provides quick, even pouring with no spillage.

Once you feel comfortable free-pouring a shot; then it is time to move on.

PREPARING DRINKS

Take one of your filled bottles and remove the pour spout. This will be your juice bottle. You can add some food coloring if you wish.

Beside it place another filled bottle fitted with a pour spout.

Fill a highball or similar glass with ice. Always make sure to pack your glasses with ice. Alcohol makes ice melt fast.

Now, pour a drink using both hands at the same time. You will have to regulate your juice pour while making sure to pour just one shot of liquor.

Practice this until you feel comfortable.

Repeat this process, switching hands used for the juice and liquor bottles.

No problem? Great. Bring out the shot and the rocks glass again. It's time to double check your liquor pour. Pour the same amount as you did for your drink into the rocks glass (no ice). Pour the liquid into the shot glass and see how you did.

A BEGINNING BARTENDER IS EASY TO SPOT. THE FIRST GIVE-AWAY IS IMPROPER BOTTLE HANDLING.

Being able to comfortably use both hands equally when bartending is the most important mechanical skill you can develop. To avoid catching "the dreaded one-handed-bartender syndrome," learn and practice two-handed bartending from the start.

A professional must be able to pour liquor and juices, use a soda gun, squeeze fruit, and straw drinks with either hand. This is necessary for speed and efficiency. Each bar that you work will be set up differently. Most will have more than one bartender. It is important that you be able to adapt for both right- and left-hand placements.

HINTS FOR LEARNING TWO-HANDED POURING

Make a conscious effort from the beginning to use and develop your weak pouring hand.

Wherever the bottle, juice, or soda gun is located, use your closest hand to pour it. Do not favor one hand over the other.

Always use both hands when pouring a mixed drink.

Pour the liquor and mixer at the same time. Concentrate on pouring the proper amount of alcohol while regulating your juice or soda pour to match your liquor pouring time.

The most important thing to remember is not to over-pour or under-pour while trying to keep up with a fast- or slow-pouring mixer. Each hand must pour independently of the other.

POURING TWO LIQUORS

When a drink calls for two or more liquors — hold a bottle in each hand and pour them at the same time.

Cut your pouring time in half so that your combined pour equals one controlled shot.

When your customer asks you to make a favorite concoction —
one shot of this, two shots of that, etc., it usually means: one part this,
two parts that, etc. When you do make a multi-shot drink, be sure to
let your customer know the cost before making it.

TIPS FOR POURING DRINKS

When making more than one drink at a time, ice and group all glasses
together that will contain the same liquor.

Remember — When a shot contains two or more liquors, the sum of
the liquors used should not exceed the amount poured for a single
shot unless you are charging accordingly.

When pouring hot liquids into glasses that are not heat treated, put a
metal spoon into the glass before you pour. The spoon will conduct
the heat and protect the glass from breaking.

Shots containing liquor only are usually served in a shot glass. Shots
that contain juices or other mixers should be served in a rocks glass
or in a glass that allows enough room for the right proportions of alcohol
and mix.

When pouring a batch of mixed shots using a strainer, group all the
glasses together and touching. Pour a little into each glass. Repeat
this process until all the glasses are evenly filled and your cocktail
shaker is empty. This method ensures that each drink is thoroughly
mixed and equal in size.

When pouring liquor into a snifter, many people prefer to stand the
glass on its side and pour the liquor until it reaches the rim of the
glass. Because of the difference in glass sizes, this will not always
give you an accurate pour. But, since many bars do not use pour
spouts with top shelf liquors, this pouring technique may give you a
more accurate pour than free pouring a bottle without a pour spout.

POUSSE-CAFÉ / LAYERED DRINKS

Pousse-Cafés are layered drinks created by floating liquors of different densities and colors atop each other. When properly poured and presented, a pousse-café allows a bartender to create and design an individual, colorful, dramatic, and tasty concoction likely to impress any customer.

Pousse-cafés can be served in any small glass that will show off its layers. If your bar does not stock special pousse-café glasses, use a shot or sherry glass. Avoid using a rocks glass. It is too wide to achieve a good layering affect without over-pouring.

The densities and weights of liquors are not indicated on the bottles and can vary widely from one brand to the next. Trial and error is often a necessity when determining density.

In general —

- The more sugar in the liquor, the more density or weight.
- The more alcohol, the lighter the liquor.

POURING A POUSSE-CAFÉ

The densest liquor is poured first; other liqueurs are 'floated' in succession, according to density.

Here are two ways to create a Pousse-Café —

1. To keep the layers separate, slowly pour the liquor over the back side of a bar spoon (a cherry may also be used to slow the flow).

Keep the spoon close to the inside wall of the glass as you "'float" each layer atop the other.

With practice, layering can be done easily and impressively, without the aid of a spoon.

2. Tilt the glass once you have poured the bottom liquor.

Place the tip of the pour spout against the inside wall of the glass, tipping the liquor bottle just far enough to begin a slow, even pour.

Pour against the inside wall of the tilted glass, just above the previous layer.

The wall of the glass slows and directs your pour, allowing the liquor to "float" atop the previous layer. (A process similar to the pouring of a draft beer.)

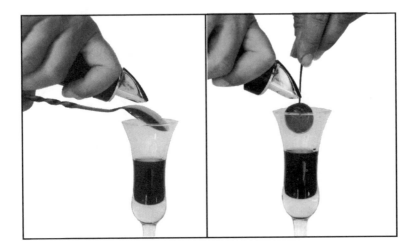

Remember —

Tilt the bottle just enough to start a slow, controlled flow.

You can also slow and adjust the flow of liquor while pouring by partially covering up the opening of your pour spout with your index finger or by slowly twisting the pour spout using an upward motion.

If you pour slowly enough against the inside wall of the glass and above the previous layer, many liquors will follow the wall and slip under the lighter layers, settling to their proper layer and correcting any misjudgments you may have made in pouring order.

Mistakes in pouring order will often correct themselves (for later use) if you let them sit in a cool place until they settle.

MAKING DRINKS

COCKTAIL SHAKERS

The Boston Shaker Set consists of two receptacles that fit together, one being a mixing glass - or Pint Glass, and the other a metal tumbler. Each can also be used separately for mixing, in conjunction with a spring coiled strainer.

Standard Shaker consists of three parts — stainless cup, lid, and strainer.

Individual Metal Tumblers are available in many sizes that fit directly over bar glasses for shaking.

 ## SHAKEN

Drinks that contain multiple ingredients or ingredients that do not mix easily are usually shaken. These include drinks containing sugar, several juices, cream or milk. Do not shake carbonated beverages.

STIRRED

Drinks that contain clear liquors or a carbonated mixer, should be stirred, not shaken. Use a mixing glass, bar spoon and strainer. Stir gently, just long enough to mix the ingredients. Over-mixing will cause loss of carbonation, melt the ice, and water down the drink. Make only the amount that you need. Strain and pour from the metal tumbler.

STRAINED

Metal strainers are designed with a flexible spring coil that fits inside the rim of mixing glasses as well as other large glasses. To keep the strainer in place while you pour, drape your index finger over the strainer top.

UP- DRINKS / CHILLED SHOTS

You may chill and serve mixed cocktails or shaken liquors in a variety of glasses. The choice of glass depends on the drink, the person, and the type or bar that you are working.

CHILLED DRINKS / PREPARING THE GLASSWARE

Chilled drinks intended for sipping include the Martini, Gibson, Gimlet, and Manhattan. These drinks should be mixed and immediately strained into a well-chilled cocktail glass to avoid a cocktail being served that is watered down with melted ice.

To chill a cocktail/martini glass —

- Fill the glass with ice and add soda water (this chills the glass evenly and quickly). Or, fill a few glasses with ice and let them sit and chill until needed.

- Let the glass chill while you prepare the cocktail.

- Empty the glass and give it a good shake to remove excess water before you pour.

Ideally, cocktail glasses should be kept chilled in a bar cooler. Unfortunately, space restrictions often don't allow this.

POURING HOT DRINKS

Whenever possible, glasses used for hot liquids should be preheated. In order to safely use glasses that are not heat-treated, place a bar spoon inside the glass prior to pouring in any hot liquid. The spoon will conduct the heat away from the glass, keeping it from cracking or exploding.

YOU CALL IT

Spirits are ordered by either generic name (Vodka, Gin, Scotch, etc.) or by brand name.

Bars use the following categories as a base for forming their price structure.

GENERIC brands are also called bar brands. They are generally inexpensive, unknown brands poured when no specific brand name is called for. These bottles are usually found in your speed rack or well area. A bartender will often be asked, "What's in your well?" This question refers to the brand name you pour when no specific one is requested. Well brands are chosen by the house, taking liquor quality, price, and house image into consideration.

PREMIUM is a term used by some bars to create a price category containing certain call brands whose costs are somewhat lower than those of the upper end call brands. (This is a category used for pricing only; cost does not always reflect the quality of a product.)

CALL liquors refer to the liquor poured when a customer requests a specific brand or "calls out" for a brand name.

TOP SHELF/SUPER PREMIUM refers to high quality, expensive liquors, usually displayed on the top shelf of the bar (Grand Marnier, B&B, Cognac, etc.).

KNOW YOUR PRODUCTS

You cannot successfully sell what you don't know. Learn as much as you can about your products, educate your wait staff, and suggest new items to your customers.

FERMENTATION AND DISTILLATION

FERMENTATION AND DISTILLATION

All alcoholic beverages fall into one of three categories —

Fermented Beverages are mixtures produced from grains or fruits such as grapes. (i.e. beer, wine)

Distilled Spirits result from a pure distillation of fermented beverages. (i.e. Vodka, Rum, Gin)

Blended or Compounded Drinks are mixtures of spirits and/or a fermented beverage with added flavorings. (i.e. liqueurs, aperitifs)

FERMENTATION

Fermentation is the basic process for making any alcoholic drink. It is a reaction created when yeast cells combine with the natural sugars found in grapes, sugarcane, or other converted grains.

Sugar + Yeast = Alcohol + Carbon Dioxide (CO_2)

The fermentation process produces liquids of low alcohol content such as beer and wine. The alcohol content becomes higher when these fermented liquids are passed through the process known as distillation.

DISTILLATION

Distillation is the method used to separate alcohol from a fermented liquid through vaporization and condensation. Distillation must be both gentle and controllable so as not to destroy the elements that distinguish fine spirits.

Distillation occurs when the fermented beverage is boiled into vapor. Alcohol vaporizes before water; or has a lower boiling point than water. Heating just above the boiling point of alcohol and below the boiling point of water makes it possible to separate the two.

As the alcohol vaporizes, it leaves the original liquid behind, taking on only the "spirit" from the grains, fruits, and other flavoring agents used in the original fermented liquid. Thus, the name "spirits" evolved.

These flavoring agents are called congeners.

The vapor cools into a liquid with a higher alcoholic co
original beverage.

Distillation takes place in stills of all shapes and sizes, ea
different flavors and characteristics.

TYPES OF STILLS

The two types of stills used most frequently in the production of spirits
are the **copper pot still** and the **continuous still**, also called the
Coffey, or patent still.

The Copper Pot Still consists of a large copper pot with a bowl-like,
rounded bottom and a long, tapered neck. The flavors of the distillate
are greatly influenced by the shape of the pot still.

Attached to the pot still is a long spiral tube surrounded by cold water.
As the vapors of the 'spirit' pass through this tube, they are condensed
to a liquid alcohol form. This somewhat inefficient distillation process
leaves behind many congeners (flavoring agents). Some are pleasant
and others not.

The art of the distillation process lies in separating the bad congeners
from the good, or, separating out the "heads and tails" which are the first
and last parts of the distillate. This leaves behind the mellower "heart" of
the spirit.

The still is refilled using only the "heart", and the process begins anew.
This process is very labor intensive. Therefore, pot stills are used only
for the finest and most expensive spirits. The best known pot-distilled
spirits are Single Malt Whisky, Cognac, and some Irish Whisky, although
other premium spirits are now turning to this distillation process.

The Continuous Still was invented in the early 19th century by an Irish
man named Coffey. This continuous, or double-column still, is more
productive than a pot still, allowing for the continuous addition of liquid
to be distilled.

The continuous still traps the vapors of a distillation inside the still so
that the vapor is continuously re-distilled until the proper level of alcohol
is achieved. This is a very efficient process and few congeners remain
behind. Most products of this process are neutral and may have flavors
added through infusions or macerations (see page 26).

TYPES OF DISTILLED SPIRITS

POTABLE SPIRITS (drinkable) spirits are spirits that take on the original flavorings of the solids used in the distillation process. These solids include grains, fruits, sugarcane and minerals. Such flavorings give each spirit its individual qualities.

NEUTRAL SPIRITS are colorless and carry no distinct taste or smell. They are alcohol distilled from grain at a high temperature, creating spirits of 190 proof or more (95% alcohol). Neutral spirits are used for blended whiskies and for making Vodka and Gin, where raw spirits are diluted down to a potable form.

Spirits mature or improve as long as they are stored in porous containers, usually wood casks. Once sealed and bottled, the spirits will not change. A bottle of 12-year-old Scotch will not improve with additional years.

FLAVORING METHODS

Infusion - Flavorings, fruits, and/or herbs are steeped in alcohol to produce many of the flavored spirits and Vodkas on the market today.

Maceration - The distilled spirit steeps with flavorings for a period of time, often months. This process imparts the strong and sometime bitter flavors of the fruit or herb used.

Distillation - The flavorings are placed in the still and are distilled along with the spirit.

Percolation - Flavoring agents are placed inside the still, usually on a screen or net. As the distillate is heated, the steam passes through these agents, capturing these often intense aromas and flavors.

PROOF

Proof is the traditional measurement of strength or alcohol content contained in a spirit. In the United States, proof is determined by doubling the percentage of alcohol contained.
For example: A spirit containing 40% alcohol is 80-proof.

Back in the early days when people were making and selling their own alcoholic beverages, there was often concern for just how much alcohol was in them. A qualitative test was developed. A sample of the alcoholic beverage was poured onto some black powder and an attempt was made to ignite the powder. If the liquid had too much water in it, the powder would not ignite. If the powder did ignite, this was "proof" that it had a high enough alcohol content.

SPIRITS

BASIC SPIRITS

BRANDY

Brandy is the general name given to a potable spirit (spirits produced at a drinkable proof) distilled from wine or a fermented fruit mash. If the fruit is grapes, it is called brandy. If it is derived from another single fruit, the name of the fruit must precede the word "brandy."

Armagnac and Cognac are two specific types of brandy named for their points of origin in France.

ARMAGNAC: A high quality brandy produced only in the Armagnac region of France, Armagnac is distilled once in a continuous copper still and aged in local oak casks. Most Armagnacs are blends, but unlike Cognac, single vintage and vineyard batches are available. The categories used for labeling Armagnac are the same as those used for Cognac.

The region of Armagnac is divided into three areas —

Bas-Armagnac is the highest quality, followed by Tenareze and Haut-Armagnac. A bottle not specifying any region is a blend of two or all three regions.

COGNAC: The best known type of Brandy. Cognac is a fine brandy made from the fermented juice of whole grapes, grown only in the Cognac district of France. Cognac is double-distilled in copper pot stills; only the heart (middle) of the second distillation is used for the Cognac. The resulting spirits produced at the beginning and the end of the distillation process (called "heads" and "tails") are removed. The remainder is then aged in white oak casks for a minimum of two and a half years. Unlike Single Malt Scotch, Cognacs are usually blends from more than one vintage and growing area.

Some brandies and Cognacs are labeled by letters —

C	=	Cognac
E	=	Especial
F	=	Fine
O	=	Old
P	=	Pale
S	=	Superior
V	=	Very
X	=	Extra

V.S. generally denotes Cognac aged an average of 5 to 9 years.
V.S.O.P. is generally aged 12 to 20 years.

Some Cognacs are labeled by stars ***. Neither labeling practice is strictly controlled. Labeling is up to each individual producer and usually shows the difference in quality of products within each brand only.

FRUIT BRANDIES: To bear this name, fruit brandies produced in the U.S. must be made with a wine-brandy base, have a specific amount of sugar and be at least 70 proof. Fruit brandies are usually of high quality and not as sweet as fruit liquors.

Some examples of fruit brandies are —

Calvados- French apple brandy
Grappa- Italian brandy made from the pomace (pulp and stems) of the wine press.
Kirschwasser- cherry brandy
Slivovitz- plum brandy
Poire Williams- French brandy made from Williams pears
Eau de vie is the French term for colorless fruit brandy.

GIN

Gin is produced using a continuous still - made by the distillation or redistillation of high-proof neutral spirits with juniper berries, herbs, roots and other flavorings. Gin requires little aging.

There are two types of gin —

Dry gin (American and English) is light and dry with a delicate flavor, making them the best gins for mixing cocktails.

Dutch gin is full-flavored with a complex, malty aroma and taste, usually served straight.

The majority of "house" gins are produced by redistilling the base spirit with juniper berries and other botanicals.

Premium gin products receive their flavor through a unique process of redistillation. As the alcohol vapors rise, they pass through a suspended mesh chamber containing the dried juniper and other botanicals.

RUM

The majority of rum is produced in the Caribbean Islands. Each island produces a rum of distinct flavor and style.

Rum is distilled from the fermented juice of sugar cane. The cane is pressed to extract its juices which are then boiled, clarified, and spun in machines that crystallize and separate the sugar from the remaining product, called molasses. The molasses is mixed with water and yeast, fermented, then distilled into rum.

Light Rum is produced in continuous stills, usually charcoal filtered and sometimes aged in oak casks. Light rum ranges in color from clear to pale gold, most are light bodied (Bacardi).

Dark Rum is full-bodied with a rich, often sweet, distinct, molasses flavor. Premium dark rum is mainly produced in pot stills and aged in oak casks for several years. The color in dark rum ranges from amber to brown and results from the addition of caramel coloring or from the cask aging of the rum.

Spiced Rum can be white, gold or dark. These rums receive their flavors through the infusion of spices, caramel and/or fruit flavors.

Añejo or aged Rum is blended from different batches or vintages. Age labeled rum usually states the age of the youngest rum used in the blend.

Cachaça (ka-shah-sa) is a Brazilian "cousin" of rum distilled from straight sugar cane.

TEQUILA / MEZCAL

Tequila and Mezcal are spirits distilled from the sap of the Mezcal Agave plant. The Mezcal plant is not a cactus, as many believe. It belongs to the Amaryllis family. Legally, in order to bear the name "Tequila", it must be produced in Mexico.

Tequila is made only from the blue Agave plant, thought to be the best Mezcal plant for Tequila production.

To produce this spirit, the heart of the agave plant is baked in steam ovens to remove the sap. The sap is fermented, mixed with additional fresh sap, and fermented again. The resulting product, called "pulque" (wine), is then double-distilled in a copper pot still.

Mezcal is produced in many regions throughout Mexico. It may be made with any variety of the agave and is baked in underground ovens fueled by wood, which imparts a somewhat smoky flavor. Its production is not quality controlled by the Mexican government. Some mezcal is produced with an agave root worm in the bottle. The past few years have brought an increasing number of high end Mezcals to the market.

The tequila market is growing rapidly, producing a standard product used for well drinks and 100% agave tequila for premium consumption.

Standard tequila may have as much as 49% additional sugars added, which can be cane sugar or corn syrup. Most standard gold tequila and Mezcal are colored by the addition of caramel, where higher quality brands receive coloring by barrel aging.

TYPES OF TEQUILA

Añejo (aged) Tequila has been aged for at least one year in seasoned oak. Its production is governed and controlled.

Blanco / White Tequila can be bottled straight from the still and, like gold tequila, is not giverment controlled.

Gold Tequila production is not legally controlled. The gold color may be the result of aging or a result of the coloring agents added by its producers.

Reposado (rested) Tequila must spend at least two months in oak barrels. It's production is governed and controlled.

Silver Tequila is a young, light-tasting, colorless Tequila, aged in wax-lined vats.

VODKA

The name Vodka comes from the Russian word *voda*, meaning "water". Most Vodkas are distilled from grains of rye, wheat, corn or potatoes. Grains used vary from brand to brand. Vodkas can be distilled in a pot or column still, depending on quality and desired tastes. It is the grains used, the production method, and water purity, that set one Vodka apart from another.

Vodka is distilled at a high proof (at least 190 proof) to remove congeners (the flavors that are carried with the alcohol through distillation). The spirit is reduced in proof (made potable) by the addition of pure water. The mixture is then filtered through charcoal-filled tanks to further purify the distillate.

Traditional Vodka produced in a column or continuous still is colorless, and neutral in taste and smell. Some premium brands acquire individual and distinct characteristics through brand-unique distillation and filtration. Vodka distilled in a pot still (as used for Cognac) will retain some aromas, flavors, and congeners from the distillate and require additional distillations to refine the product.

Some popular Vodkas and their specific characteristics:

> **Absolut** - Sweden, Winter Wheat
> **Belvedere** - Poland, Rye
> **Chopin** - Poland, Potato
> **Finlandia**- Finland, Barley
> **Grey Goose** - France, Mixed Grains
> **Ketel One** - Holland, Wheat
> **Pearl** - Canada, Winter Wheat
> **Skyy** - America, Mixed Grain
> **Smirnoff** - America, Mixed Grain
> **Stolichnaya** - Russia, Winter Wheat
> **Tanquery Sterling** - England, Mixed Grain
> **Vox** - Netherlands, Wheat

Distillation types and amounts vary too much to be included.

WHISKEY / WHISKY

The word "whisky" comes from the Celtic word meaning "water of life." Both Scotch and Canadian whisky are spelled without the "e". Whiskey is distilled from grain. Originally, distillers used the grains that were most available, inexpensive and abundant to their area. These different grains, flavorings, and blends give each area's whiskey a distinct style, flavor, and color.

BLENDED WHISKEY is a blend of at least 20% straight whiskey (see page 34) mixed with neutral grain spirits. The blend is typically light, soft and mild and can consist of more than twenty single malts. The exact blends are guarded trade secrets.

Blended whiskey and Bourbon are interchangeable in recipes. Depending on your geographical area, you may be pouring either when a customer asks for "whiskey" without specifying Scotch, Bourbon, or straight whisky. Blended whiskies are predominantly used on the east coast, whereas Bourbon is most often poured as the well whiskey on the west coast. Crown Royal is one popular brand.

BOURBON WHISKEY was first distilled in Bourbon County, Kentucky, where corn was more plentiful than rye, but it can be produced anywhere in the U.S. It is distilled from a grain mash containing at least 51% corn but not more than 79%.

Bourbon is a straight whiskey, which means that it contains no additives, apart from the water used to reduce the proof, and has not been blended. Bourbon must be distilled at 160 proof or less and aged for a minimum of two years in new, charred-oak barrels. Some call brands are Jim Beam, Early Times, Old Grand-Dad, and Old Crow.

Small Batch Bourbon is a blended from a limited number of selected oak charred barrels chosen by the distiller. Two examples are Blantons and Knob Creek.

CANADIAN WHISKY is distilled from corn, rye, wheat, and barley malt. None of these ingredients may exceed more than 50%. Canadian whisky is a blended, light-bodied whisky with a more delicate flavor than American whiskey. Some call brands are Crown Royal, Seagram's V.O., and Canadian Club (C.C.).

IRISH WHISKEY is distilled from a mash of barley, corn, rye, wheat, and oats. The barley malt, unlike the whisky of Scotland, is dried in closed kilns, which eliminates the smoky, peaty flavor found in Scotch. Bushmill's and Jameson are two examples.

RYE WHISKEY is distilled from a mash of at least 51% rye. Rye whiskies are not very common. Seagram's V.O. and C.C. are often mistakenly called rye. They are actually a blended whiskey. An example of true "rye" is Old Overholt.

SOUR MASH WHISKEY is usually a type of Bourbon. It differs from other whiskies because a portion of the mash used in the distillation process is "sour," or spent, meaning that it has been used during a previous distillation. Fresh mash is added to the "sour," creating a unique flavor of whiskey.

STRAIGHT WHISKEY is any grain whiskey that has not been blended with any other whiskey or neutral grain spirit. "Straight" whiskey must be distilled from at least a 51% base of a single type of grain.

TENNESSEE WHISKEY is similar to Bourbon, but is filtered through maple charcoal. Made only in Tennessee, it must be made from at least 51% of one particular grain (usually corn). Jack Daniel's and George Dickel are two well known brands.

SCOTCH WHISKY

Today, the majority of Scotch whisky sold is a blend of malt and grain whisky. Originally whiskies were either malt or straight grain. Blending the two together produced a lighter, smoother product that appealed to more people than the original, full-bodied, unblended Scotch whisky. This scotch is often referred to as American Whisky. Blended Scotch whisky contains a mix of copper-pot distilled malts mixed with whisky made from continuous stills.

There are several determining factors responsible for the distinct differences in flavor and bouquet found among the Scotches. These factors include: local water, peat, climate, the wood casks used for aging along with the design of the still.

By law, Scotch whisky must be both distilled and aged in Scotland for at least three years, and it cannot enter the U.S. unless aged for four years. Scotch is usually aged in oak casks that once held bourbon, wine, or sherry.

SCOTCH MALT WHISKY contains no grain whisky. It can be single malt or blended malt. Malt whisky is full-bodied, high in quality, and usually aged longer than whiskies containing grain.

VATTED MALT WHISKY is a blend of malt whiskies from different distilleries and contains no grain alcohol.

SINGLE MALT SCOTCH WHISKY

The oldest of todays Scottish distilleries date back to the 1700's.

Single malt Scotch is an unblended Scotch whisky distilled in a traditional copper pot still from malted (germinated) barley only, and produced by a single distillery. The age on the label represents the youngest malt contained in the bottle.

The smoky, peaty characteristics of Scotch are derived when the germinated barley is dried on screens directly over a fire fueled by local peat. Other Scotches receive their peat from the local water supply that carries with it the taste and smell of the area's peat. Many Scotches draw from both processes.

The interest in and consumption of single malt Scotch has risen over the last few years. Many people are exploring the world of single malts in much the same way they explore new wines: tasting for body, bouquet, palate and finish.

Single malts are meant to be served at room temperature in order to fully appreciate the flavor, aroma and color of the malt. Some say adding a splash of two of water will release the aroma.

Proper glassware is necessary to fully appreciate the complexities of Single malts. Single malt glasses resemble a tall, narrow snifter, flared at the top. Traditional brandy snifters, although handy, bring out the alcohol and mask the actual aroma of the malt. If you don't have traditional malt glasses (which are usually crystal), Scotch enthusiasts will appreciate service neat in a rocks glass, although less educated consumers will be turned off by this presentation. Best to use your judgement. When in doubt, serve in a snifter. Never serve single malts in a shot glass!

To educate yourself and your customers try this:
Place a shot of single malt in a brandy snifter. Put your nose to the snifter and smell the aroma. Now, pour the shot into a rocks glass and smell again. The difference is remarkable.

Like fine wine, the taste of single malts reflects their points of origin.

THE HIGHLANDS region is Scotland's largest whisky-producing district. It encompasses a broad area that can further be broken down into individual sections, each producing malts with diverse qualities. Highland malts are generally light-bodied, fruity, and somewhat sweet with a medium smoky flavor.

The Speyside section of the Highlands is considered one of the premier Scotch whisky-producing areas in the world. Speyside malts are big and complex, often with a sherry finish.

THE LOWLANDS generally produce the lightest malts, both in flavor and color. They are sweet, soft and fruity.

CAMBLETOWN malts receive much of their character from the sea air, producing a full bodied, complex, malt..

ISLANDS

> The isle of Skye, Mull and Jura produce full-bodied, peaty, malts, with the sea air lending them a somewhat salty flavor.
>
> **ISLAY** (pronounced eye-luh) malts are very distinct. They are full-bodied, intensely peaty, somewhat salty, with a strong, smoky flavor.

OTHER SPIRITS, LIQUEURS AND CORDIALS

~ proofs (°) given are approximate ~

The words Liqueur and Cordial are used interchangeably in the U.S.. Liqueurs were first developed by the Christian monks of the middle ages to help the sick. The monks added secret combinations of honey, seeds, herbs, spices, roots, and bark to distilled-base spirits and offered them as remedies.

A **liqueur** or **cordial** is a sweet alcoholic beverage, often flavored with fruits, herbs, or spices, and sometimes cream.

ABSINTHE: A green liqueur with a bitter, licorice flavor. Prepared from the wormwood plant. Once thought to be a narcotic, it was banned by the U.S. government. Made now minus the wormwood and marketed under the trade names — Pernod and Herbsaint.

ADVOKATT: An eggnog liqueur originally from Holland. Made from neutral spirits, egg yolks and sugar. 40°

AKVAVIT / AQUAVIT: A neutral spirit redistilled with caraway. This Scandinavian spirit is usually served cold. 80°

AMARETTO: An almond-flavored liquor made from apricot pits. 50°

AMER PICON: An orange-flavored French apéritif made with quinine and spices. 78°

ANISETTE: A licorice-flavored liqueur made from anise seed. 60°

BÉNÉDICTINE: A Cognac base blended with a secret herb formula. First made by the Bénédictine monks in France. 86°

B&B: A mix of Bénédictine and brandy. 86°

BITTERS: A concentrated flavoring agent made from roots, berries, herbs and plants. Often used as an aid to digestion when served with soda. 80°

CHAMBORD: A French liqueur made from black raspberries. 33°

CAMPARI: An Italian apéritif, bitter in taste, usually served over ice with soda and lime. 48°

CHARTREUSE: A spicy, herb-flavored, brandy-based liqueur, available in both green and yellow. Green is dryer then yellow. Yellow 80° - Green

COINTREAU: An orange-flavored, high-quality liqueur made from the skins of curaçao oranges. Cointreau is a brand name for this fine Triple Sec. 80°

CRÈME LIQUEURS:
Crème de Cacao - cacao and vanilla beans (dark and light).
Crème de Cassis - black currants
Crème de Menthe - mint (green and white)

CURAÇAO: An orange-flavored liqueur made from dried orange peels (orange and blue). 50°

DRAMBUIE: A sweet and spicy liqueur, with a base of aged Scotch whisky. 80°

DUBONNET: A quinine-flavored aperitif wine (red and white).

FRANGELICO: A hazelnut-flavored liqueur from Italy. 56°

GALLIANO: A sweet, spicy, golden Italian liquor. 70°

GRAND MARNIER: An orange-flavored, cognac-based, French liquor. 80°

GRAPPA: An Italian grape brandy, sharp in taste, distilled from grape pomace (skin and stems).

IRISH MIST: A spicy Irish whisky flavored with honey. 80°

IRISH CREAM: Irish whisky flavored with cream, mocha, and sweeteners. The most popular brand is Bailey's.

JAGERMEISTER: A German liquor containing over forty herbs and spices. 70°

KAHLÚA: A premium coffee-flavored liquor from Mexico. 53°

KÜMMEL: A liqueur flavored with caraway and anise seeds as well as other herbs.

LILLET: A French apéritif wine (red and white).

METAXA: A Greek brandy with a rich, sweet taste.

MIDORI: A honeydew-flavored liquor from Japan. 46°

OUZO: An anise-flavored apéritif from Greece. 90°

PEPPERMINT SCHNAPPS: A light, mint-tasting liqueur with less sugar and more alcohol than Crème de Menthe. Other types include peach, spearmint, and cinnamon. 50°-107°

PERNOD: A licorice-flavored liquor. 80°

PIMM'S: A gin base with fruit flavors. 67°

SAMBUCA: A licorice-flavored Italian liqueur made from the Sambuca plant. Often served straight up in a snifter with three coffee beans. 84°

SLOE GIN: A sweet, red liqueur made from sloe berries. 50°

SOUTHERN COMFORT: Bourbon with peach liqueur and fresh peaches. 86°

STREGA: Italian liqueur made from herbs, spices, and plants.

TIA MARIA: A coffee-flavored liqueur from Jamaica. 53°

TRIPLE SEC: An orange-flavored liqueur similar to Curaçao but colorless and not as sweet. 60°

TUACA: An Italian citrus and vanilla-flavored milk brandy (contains milk). 70°

VANDERMINT: A Dutch chocolate liqueur with mint. 60°

VERMOUTH: An apéritif wine flavored with herbs. Available in two types — Dry and Sweet. 36°

WILD TURKEY: A bourbon-based liquor flavored with spices.

YUKON JACK: A Canadian whisky base flavored with citrus and herbs. 100°

BEER

A fermented beverage brewed from malted barley and flavored with hops.

LAGER BEER

Lager beers contain a small amount of hops and are delicate in flavor and aroma. They are produced by yeasts that operate best at the cool bottom part of the fermenting vessel. Lagers are lagered (stored) for several months to allow sedimentation before being packaged into bottles, cans or kegs.

BOCK: A heavy, dark, slightly sweet and strong, lager beer, brewed from caramelized malt.

DRY LAGER: Typically brewed longer than a regular lager. This causes more of the starches to convert to fermentable sugars, resulting in a less-sweet taste.

ICE LAGER: Typically brewed the same way as regular lager. During the fermentation or aging process they are frozen, creating their distinctive taste.

LIGHT BEER: A beer with fewer calories and less alcohol than regular lager. This can be done in many ways. Excess sugar can be removed from the finished beer or converted during the brewing process, and/ or carbonated water can be added to dilute the finished product.

MALT LIQUOR: Brewed using a combination of barley malt and pure starches that create a large amount of fermentable sugars in the wort. This process produces a beer with a higher amount or alcohol than a regular lager.

MÄRZEN/OCTOBERFEST: Beer originally produced in Germany during the month of March and lagered (laid down in icy cellars) for final consumption during Oktoberfest. Märzen (pronounced Mairtzen) has become a popular lager produced year round.

PILSNER: A term originally used to label beer brewed in Pilsen, Czechoslovakia. The original being Pilsner Urquell. Pilsner is a golden lager with a hint of hops, generally high in carbonation, light, bright, and dry.

ALE

Ale is a beer produced by yeasts that tends to be thicker, floating to the top of the barrel during the fermentation process. It is fermented at a higher temperature than lager and generally has a higher alcohol content. The taste is rich, fruity, full-bodied, with a somewhat bitter flavor.

CREAM ALE: Usually have s slightly sweet taste and a pale, golden color. May be specially brewed or made by blending larger with ale.

FLAVORED ALE: Flavors are added either during the brewing or aging process (honey, oatmeal, raspberry etc.).

HEFEWEIZEN: Uses wheat in conjunction with barley and/or other grains. "Hefe" refers to the white-colored yeast sediment in the wheat beer. "Weizen" is the German word for wheat. Hefe Weisse beer indicates a beer that is sedimented (cloudy with sediment remaining). They are fruity and refreshing; Usually served in a tall, vase-like glass, and garnished with a lemon wheel.

PORTER: An ale, brown in color and flavored with roasted malt. Porter has a strong bittersweet flavor.

STOUT: A dark, heavy-bodied, somewhat bitter ale. Stout offers its peak flavor when served at 55°F.

SAKE

Sake is a specialized form of beer brewed from polished rice. It is often called Japanese rice wine due to its lack of color and carbonation. There are many grades of sake determined by brewing process and the degree to which the rice has been polished down. Only the inner kernel of the rice is used. The more polished the rice, the cleaner, more refined and fragrant the flavor of the sake.

The flavor of sake is sweet and dry. Traditionally served warm to release its bouquet; Heating sake is most often a way to mask the flavors of a lower grade product. Premium sakes are meant to be served chilled to highlight their floral, fruity characteristics.

WHAT IS A MICROBREW?

At one time, microbreweries were defined as those producing under 15,000 barrels a year. However, there are now some microbreweries far exceeding that limit, causing that long-held definition to be questioned. Brew pubs share the same volume limit, but 50% or more of their production is consumed on-premise. Contract brewers are those who design the beer, stipulate the recipes, market and sell the beer, but contract another brewery to physically produce the product.

HOW BEER IS MADE

INGREDIENTS

CEREALS: Can be raw, such as corn or rice, or prepared, such as corn grits. Cereals are used along with malt to produce a milder, lighter product.

HOPS: Hops are the dried blossoms from the female hop vine. They are added to the beer for flavoring. Hops give beer its character and bitterness.

MALT: Malt is barley that has been steeped (soaked in water) and germinated (sprouted).

WATER: Beer consists of approximately 90% water. The quality of water used in the beer-making process is very important since it affects the flavor and character of product.

YEAST: Brewer's yeast is the fermenting agent that transforms the wort (the filtered liquid produced from grains and fermentable sugars) into alcohol and CO_2. Different yeast strains produce different flavors. The yeast used to produce lager beer works from the bottom. Yeast used for ale and wheat beer works from the top.

BREWING AND FERMENTING BEER

This is a brief overview of the complex process involved in the brewing and fermentation of beer. It is intended to give you a basic understanding of the process. There are many in-depth books written solely on this subject for those interested in learning more about the exact science.

The brewing process begins after the barley is malted (germinated), ground and roasted.

The resulting malt along with cereals and water is mashed in a mash tun, which dissolves any soluble materials.

The mash is transferred into a lauter tun, where the solids are broken down further by rakes. The liquid is then strained, leaving behind a clarified liquid called "wort."

Hops are added to the wort, boiled in a brewing kettle, and then removed, giving the brew its characteristic bitter flavor.

The wort is cooled and put into a fermenting vat where brewer's yeast is added to the liquid. This addition begins the fermentation process. As the yeast multiplies, it converts the sugars in the wort to alcohol and CO_2 gas.

After fermentation, the beer is filtered and aged. The CO_2 gas produced is saved and can be returned to the beer for carbonation at the end of the brewing process.

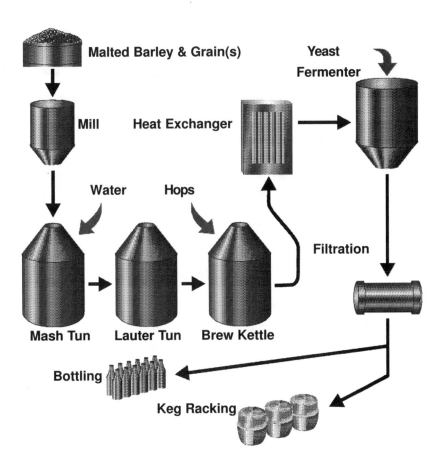

PACKAGING BEER

Draft beer, unlike canned and bottled beer, is not pasteurized. Therefore, it must be kept refrigerated to ensure freshness. The shelf-life of keg beer is somewhere around 60 days. Cans and bottled beer are pasteurized and need not be refrigerated. They should be sold within 120 days from the packaging date.

To ensure freshness, once cold, avoid warming and re-chilling all beer. Beer should not be exposed to light. Light causes beer to release sulfur, giving it a "skunky" taste. It is important to rotate the beer in your cooler, making sure that all beer served remains fresh.

Pasteurization is the process by which the bottles or cans of beer are heated for a short of time, then cooled. This process stops any additional fermentation from taking place once the beer is packaged, avoiding further production of CO_2 gas that may cause the bottles or cans of beer to burst. This process takes out any impurities that could affect the flavor or shelf-life of the product. On the downside, pasteurization does somewhat alter the fresh taste found in draft beer (which is not pasteurized).

Beer companies have found new ways to filter out remaining yeast cells without pasteurizing. This process is called cold filtration and allows the beer to be canned, bottled, and labeled as "draft" beer, while still retaining the shelf life and temperature requirements of pasteurized beer products.

DRAFT BEER

Domestic beer kegs (called ½ barrels) contain 15.5 gallons, while import kegs, in general, hold 13.2 gallons.

Note: Domestic micro-brewers often purchase used kegs, some of which may be of import size.

A domestic keg weighs about 161 lbs. and holds 1,984 liquid ounces. This is roughly equivalent to seven cases of 12-oz. bottled beer. If you are using pint (16-oz.) glasses, a keg should yield around 125+ glasses of beer, depending on the amount of head poured and the shape of the glass.

DISPENSING DRAFT BEER

When pouring a draft or bottled beer, it is important to begin with a clean glass. Any soap residue will affect the taste and carbonation of beer. Draft beer should be at the proper temperature (38°F), and set at a pressure of 12 to 14 lbs/sq. in. Have a professional clean your draft lines and check for correct pressure on a regular basis.

Position the glass directly under the pouring spigot at a 45° angle.

Open and close the spigot handle all the way, or the beer will not pour properly (a common mistake made by beginning bartenders).

Run the beer down the inside of the glass, slowly bringing it to an upright position. Adjust your pour to accommodate variations in different beers and beer systems. Beer should be served with a head of ¾ to 1 inch.

POURING HINTS FOR DRAFT BEER

If your draft system has two faucets that allow double pouring, learn how to pour two beers at a time.

Keep a glass in each hand and hold the glasses under the spigot. Use your index fingers to start the draft.

When the glass is close to full, use your index fingers to stop the beer flow.

If you need to pour more than one draft using a single spigot, use your free hand to ready the second glass.

Use your time wisely while pouring draft beer. Plan your next move, acknowledge your customers, or take another order.

SERVING HINTS FOR BOTTLED BEER

Pour bottled beer in the same manner as explained for draft beer.

When a customer asks, "What beers do you have?", save time by asking, "Domestic or Imported? - Bottle or Draft?" before reciting your full list.

Display your beer selections whenever possible. The different shaped bottles, brands, and colorful labels, along with your knowledge of product, will aid your customers in their decision.

When opening a bottled beer, hold the bottle as close to the top as possible. This creates less bottle movement and minimizes the instances of overflowing beers.

When a beer is foaming over, tilt the bottle at an angle. The foam will settle inside the curve of the bottle rather than on you.

HOW A KEG WORKS

Many beer kegs work with a single-handle, tavern head system with two lines — one line going into the keg, carrying the CO_2, and one going out of the keg, carrying the carbonated beer to the pouring spigot. As the CO_2 is introduced to the surface of the beer in the keg, its pressure forces the beer up the stainless steel probe to the pouring faucet.

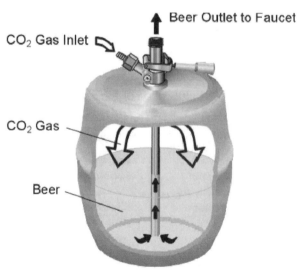

Beer Outlet to Faucet

CO_2 Gas Inlet

CO_2 Gas

Beer

CHANGING A KEG

Most new-style kegs use a single-handle tavern head tap.

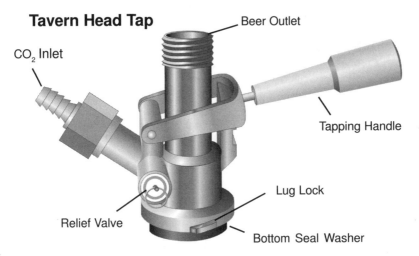

Tavern Head Tap — Beer Outlet

CO$_2$ Inlet

Tapping Handle

Lug Lock

Relief Valve

Bottom Seal Washer

1. Pull the tavern head handle out until it springs upward into the open position, signaling that the flow of beer and CO$_2$ has been shut off.

2. Turn the tavern head ¼ turn to the right, rotating the tap head past the housing locks, allowing it to be released from the keg.

3. Replace the empty keg with a full one.

4. Align the lug locks on the tap head with the housing on top of the keg. Turn the tap head ¼ turn to the left, securing it to the keg.

5. Pull the tap handle out and depress downward to the locking position. This will open the beer and CO$_2$ valves. The keg is now ready to go.

There is some natural carbonation to beer. If you roll, drop, or shake a keg, the beer will not pour properly until the foam settles.

WHAT IS CO$_2$?

Carbon Dioxide (CO$_2$) provides the push, causing beer to flow out of a keg. It is also a natural by-product of beer, making it very economical to use.

At room temperature CO$_2$ is a gas; but under high pressure and low temperatures, it converts to a liquid. When the pressurized tank is filled, about ½ is filled with liquid, while the upper ½ of the tank is filled with gas.

As the beer is drawn through the system, the liquid is continually converted to gas. The pressure in the tank will not decrease until all the CO$_2$ is used up.

Caution should be taken when handling CO$_2$ tanks —
- Keep them upright.
- Don't drop tanks.
- Don't refrigerate tanks.

Care and maintenance of your draft beer system, along with the setting of CO$_2$ pressure, should be performed only by trained individuals. In many cases, the care and maintenance of draft beer systems is the responsibility of your beer distributor.

CHANGING A CO$_2$ TANK

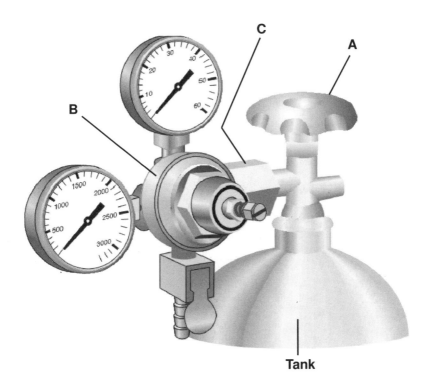

Tank

1. Turn drum valve handle (A) on top of tank (as far as it will go) to the "off" position.

2. Remove regulator (B) from empty tank by loosening the coupling nut (C) with an adjustable wrench.

3. Attach regulator to new tank by tightening the regulator coupling nut. Be sure to use a new washer if your regulator does not have a built in o-ring.

4. Turn handle on top of tank (A) (as far as it will go) to the "on" position.

WINES

WINE MAKING

Wine is the pure, naturally-fermented juice of fresh, ripe grapes. The job of the winemaker is to guide the wine's development. Ripe grapes are picked and put into a crusher-stemmer, which removes the stems and produces a grape "must." The must is pressed to separate the grape juice from the skins.

To produce red wine — the skins remain with the juice to add color during the fermentation process.

FERMENTATION OF WINE

In the final stages of ripening, yeast cells form on the skin of the grape. When the skin of the grape is broken, the yeast goes to work on the natural sugars found inside the grape. This begins the process known as fermentation.

Fermentation of wine requires a balance between the yeast and sugar contained in the grapes. Although yeast is naturally present in the grapes, it is often replaced by laboratory produced strains of pure yeast. This controlled balance (determined by the personal touch of the wine maker) results in the making of dry versus sweet wines. The fermentation process ends when the sugar supply runs out or when the concentration of alcohol overpowers the remaining yeast cells.

STILL WINES

WINE NAMES

Regional names are used for European wines. These wines are named for the region in which they are produced. Burgundy, Chianti, and Rhine are examples of regional names. These names may also be used to categorize wines from other areas; in this case, the regional name is not capitalized (burgundy, chianti, rhine, etc.).

Burgundy represents one of the most important wine regions in France; producing the red grape of Pinot Noir and the white grape of Chardonnay. French Burgundy is some of the finest wine in the world.

In the United States, however, the term burgundy is most often used to describe wine in generic terms. Both Chardonnay and Pinot Noir are bottled in a burgundy style bottle that is wide and bowed.

Varietal names are commonly used for wines made in the United States. In order to use a varietal name the wine must be made with at least 75% of the grape type used in the name. These names include: Chardonnay, Cabernet Savignon, Pinot Noir, etc.

Generic wines are made with any grape(s) that the producer chooses; they are often sold in large jugs or boxes and served as "house wines" under the generic names burgundy, chablis, claret, and rhine.

When generic names are used domestically, the place of production must also appear on the label (e.g., California Chablis).

Proprietary names are created by the winery for the marketing of their wines. These names are often used to describe a wine's specific attributes or uniqueness (e.g., Hearty Burgundy).

Wines produced in the United States are identified primarily by grape type. California produces the most popular American wines, wines that rival and often times surpass the quality of European wines. Many other states including Washington, Oregon, and New York also produce good quality wines.

WHITE WINES

CHARDONNAY: Burgundy type. A dry, rich, full-bodied wine. Most Chardonnay receives some oak treatment either during or after the fermentation process The better Chardonnays are aged in French oak barrels (which can cost up to $600 each).

GEWÜRZTRAMINER: Rhine or Alsatian type. A highly aromatic, light-bodied, spicy wine. Tastes can range from dry to sweet.

PINOT BLANC: A dry crisp, medium bodied wine with high acidity and low sugar content.

PINOT GRIS/PINOT GRIGIO: Pinot Gris (gray Pinot) is a medium-to-full bodied wine with low acidity.

RIESLING: Rhine or Alsatian type. A light-bodied, fragrant and fruity wine - can be sweet or dry.

SAUVIGNON BLANC: Also called Fumé Blanc. Fruity, dry, crisp, light to medium-bodied with herbaceous characteristics (often called grassy).

VIOGNIER: A grape from France's Rhone Valley. Floral, low acidity, medium-to-full-bodied and gaining popularity in California.

RED WINES

Red grape varieties differ from one another through their aroma, flavor, alcohol content, and levels of tannin. Tannin is an astringent substance found in the grape skins, seeds, stems, and oak barrels used for aging.

CABERNET SAUVIGNON: A deep-colored, medium- to full-bodied wine. Cabernet Sauvignon is fairly tannic and is often blended with other less tannic grapes to produce a softer wine.

CLARET: A dry, tart wine with medium color and body. Claret is a generic term used to describe red wine similar to the type made in Bordeaux.

CHIANTI: Italian type. A dry, full-bodied, slightly tart wine.

MERLOT: A soft, full bodied, spicy wine, often used as a blend to soften Cabernet Sauvignon. Merlot is deep in color, low in tannin, and high in alcohol.

PINOT NOIR: A light-to medium-bodied wine with a medium-to-high acidity and medium-low tannin. Its aroma can be very fruity (red berries) or earthy.

ROSÉ: These wines are classified as red wines. The individual coloring of these wines is determined by the length of time that the grape skins are allowed to remain in contact with the juice during fermentation.

SANGIOVESE: An Italian grape with growing popularity in California. A fruity cherry flavor and aroma, can vary from light-to-full bodied, is medium-to-high in acid, and medium in tannin.

SYRAH/SHIRAZ: Syrah is a full bodied, deeply colored wine. Called Shiraz in Australia with numerous styles ranging from full to light in body and color, with flavors of fresh strawberries.

ZINFANDEL: A rich, deeply colored wine with a spicy, berry-like taste and smell. Medium to high in tannins with a high alcohol content.

FORTIFIED WINES

Fortified wine contains brandy or other spirits added to stop the fermentation process or to increase the alcohol content.

MADEIRA: Produced on the island on Madeira, off the coast of Portugal. Madeira wines are fortified with locally produced brandy.

MARSALA: An Italian fortified wine similar to Maderia.

PORT: Produced originally in Portugal. Any port produced and bottled in Portugal and shipped to the U.S. must be labeled "Porto".

Port is made by adding brandy to wine that is still in the fermentation process. This raises the alcohol content and stops fermentation. The unfermented grape sugar remains in the wine, resulting in a sweet, fortified wine.

TYPES OF PORT

VINTAGE PORT: A port that is determined by the winemakers to be from an exceptional year. It must be bottled within two years, then aged in the bottle for between 8 to 20 years. The bottles are "laid down" on their sides for aging. During this time, Vintage Port develops a heavy deposit or crust inside the bottle. Vintage ports are rich and tannic and should be decanted before drinking.

Store Vintage Port on its side, in a cool area, and serve at room temperature.

LATE BOTTLED VINTAGE PORT (LBV): A port from a specific vintage, but not usually a top year. LBV is aged in wood for four to six years before being bottled and requires no bottle aging. Generally full-bodied and moderately priced.

RUBY PORT: A bright, fruity, ruby-colored young port, aged in wood for a relatively short amount of time. *Reserve* or *Special Reserve* ruby ports are aged longer.

TAWNY PORT: Aged in wood casks, opposed to the bottle-aging of vintage port. Tawny port is repeatedly "fined," a process that removes any crust or deposits in the wine. This process, along with oxidation during wood aging, causes the port to take on a tawny color. The longer it is aged, the paler the color and the drier the Tawny. The better tawnies will bear an age on their labels which represents the average age of wines blended to make the port.

WHITE PORT: Made exclusively from white grapes and aged in wood for a relatively short time. White port is generally softer and drier than other ports.

There are many new and exciting domestic ports on the market today.

SHERRY

Jerez de la Frontera is the Spanish town at the center of sherry production. Unlike that of port, the fermentation process is allowed to continue until the sugar supply runs out. The sherry is then fortified with locally produced grape brandy and aged in oak casks. The various degrees of sweetness and depth of color are the results of specific blending by individual shippers.

TYPES OF SHERRY

There are two types of sherry — **Fino** and **Oloroso.**

FINO: A pale, light, dry sherry with medium body, produced when "flor," a wine-yeast, develops on top during production.

> **Mansanilla:** A pale, very dry, fino-type sherry, produced in the coastal town of Sanlúcar de Barramesa, where the salt air influences its light, tart flavor and fragrance.

> **Amontillado:** A pale to light gold colored, full-bodied, dry fino with a nutty flavor.

OLOROSO: A deep golden, full-bodied, nutty sherry produced when "flor" (wine yeast) does not develop. Oloroso is the basis for sweeter sherries often known as cream and brown sherries.

AROMATIZED WINES

Aromatized wine is fortified wine that has been steeped with herbs, roots, flowers or other flavoring agents. Aromatized wines include apéritifs and vermouths.

APÉRITIFS

The term apéritif comes from the Latin word *aperio*, meaning "to open." Apéritifs are light spirits intended "to open up the appetite," but can also be enjoyed on their own anytime.

POPULAR APÉRITIFS

CAMPARI: Usually served over ice with soda and garnished with a wedge of lime.

LILLÉT: (red and white) Served over ice and garnished with an orange slice or peel.

DUBONNET: (red and white) Keep refrigerated and serve chilled.

VERMOUTH: This aromatized wine is available in both dry and sweet varieties. Two popular brands are Martini & Rossi and Cinzano.

Dry Vermouth is the flavoring ingredient in Martinis and Gibsons. Sweet Vermouth is the flavoring ingredient in Manhattans.

Other apéritifs include Pernod, Ouzo and Amer Picon.

CHAMPAGNE / SPARKLING WINES

Champagne and sparkling wines have much the same relationship as brandy and Cognac. In France, only sparkling wine that comes from the region of Champagne may be labeled "Champagne."

Champagne is made from fully ripe red or white grapes. The wine intended for champagne is bottled before fermentation is complete. The "sparkle" or carbon dioxide may be formed naturally or added artificially.

Blanc de Blancs — Made from the juice of white grapes only

Rosé or Pink — Produced by adding small amounts of red wine

Brute — Very dry

Extra Sec/Extra Dry — Dry

Sec or Dry — Slightly sweet

Demi-Sec — Sweet

Doux — Very sweet

GLASSWARE

A customer's first impression of a drink is determined by the glass in which it is served. The taste of a cocktail is enhanced when presented in a sparkling clean glass that says "drink me!"

GLASSWARE

The definition of appropriate glassware has changed over the years, giving way to multipurpose glassware suitable for a variety of cocktails.

Champagne, cocktail and wine are a few examples of glasses known as stemware. Stemware is designed to be carried and served with your hand on the stem, not on the bowl of the glass. This service keeps the warmth of your hand from altering the temperature of the glass and its contents. It also keeps the glass free of fingerprints.

Cocktail or Martini Glass
Use this glass for cocktails served chilled and strained.
Chill the glass before using.

Rocks Glass / Old Fashioned Glass
Use either glass for drinks served over ice or chilled shots
containing juices

Highball Glass
Use for standard drinks containing soda or water.

Double Rocks / Bucket Glass
A popular glass used for "double" drinks and for drinks containing juices. Often used by bars instead of a highball glass.

Collins Glass
Used for Collins drinks and for drinks requested "tall."

Zombie / Poco Grande / Hurricane

Multipurpose specialty glasses. Used for enhancing the presentation of a variety of cocktails including Bloody Marys, Rum punches and blended drinks.

Wine Glasses

Universal glass - Red Wine - White Wine

Champagne Tulip / Flute Glass

Brandy Snifter

Used for brandy (straight and flavored) and assorted liquors served "up," heated, or mixed with hot water. The design allows the hand to cradle the glass, warm its contents, and release its bouquet.

Cordial Glass / Sherry Glass

Used for layering drinks and serving cordials, especially those accompanying coffee service. A brandy snifter is often used in place of a cordial glass (except for layered drinks).

Coffee Glass

Used for fizzes and coffee drinks served with whipped cream.

Single Malt Glass

Use this glass for serving single malt whisky neat. The fluted top allows the flavor to come through above the alcohol.

Fiesta Grande Glass

Use this glass for frozen drinks.

Shot Glass

Use these glasses for serving shots that do not contain juice or mixers. Can also be used to serve layered drinks.

ICE

ICE

Ice used in cocktails must be clean and fresh. Clean your ice bin on a regular basis. If your bar uses soda guns, you may have a cold plate sitting on the bottom of your ice bin. This plate serves to chill the soda as it flows through to the soda guns. Many a science project has been known to flourish under this plate. Known in the business as "bar slime," it develops fast, so keep a handle on it.

Ice machines are equipped with a sensor probe usually located on the top inside of the machine above the ice. This probe signals the machine when to produce more ice or shut down when full.

Know where the probe is located in each machine that you use (top right, left, or middle). Always be sure to take your ice from around the probe and redistribute the remaining ice evenly. If you fail to do this, your machine will be fooled into believing that it is full when the only ice remaining may be piled up in one spot around the probe.

Rules for ice bins —

- When filling a glass, always use an ice scoop!!

- Use your ice bin for ice only.

- Keep bottles and juices in a separate iced compartment.

BROKEN GLASS

Know that a glass will break in your ice only at the busiest of times (bartenders' karma).

When a glass is broken in or around your ice, take no chances!

If you find all the pieces and can recreate the entire glass without any minute missing chips, consider yourself extremely lucky. If not, get out the buckets and start scooping!

Empty all of your ice and flush the bin with hot water. Check and clean the surrounding area for any glass that may have strayed (slivers of glass easily attach to, and can be dropped from bottles and juice containers into your new ice. Wet some bar naps to pick up slivers).

Important: **The only way to ensure customer safety and minimize bar liability is to remove all potentially contaminated ice and rinse out your ice bin immediately.**

DRINK GARNISHES

A garnish is used to flavor or decorate a drink.

GARNISHES

In order to ensure freshness —

- Prepare garnishes as close to serving time as possible.
- Use a sharp knife and a clean cutting board.
- Cut lemon and lime wedges large enough to grasp and squeeze.

Garnishes talk —

Using old or small garnishes will make customers question the quality of their drinks. **WASH ALL FRUIT BEFORE CUTTING!!**

LIMES

Limes are served with drinks containing tonic (Vodka, Rum, Gin) and with many drinks containing soda. Margaritas and non-fruit daiquiris also require limes.

When you squeeze a lime into a drink, shield the top of the glass with your free hand. Keep the juice in the glass, where it belongs.

To cut a lime —

1. Cut the "knobs" off from the ends of the lime.
2. Slice the lime in half, lengthwise into 2 parts.
3. Cut lengthwise, down the center of each half, making 4 parts.
4. Cut crosswise to make from six to eight wedges per half.

OR

Cut each of the four parts again lengthwise making eight long wedges. Cut a vertical slit about half way down the inside wedge, allowing it to be hung on the rim of the glass for garnish.

LEMONS

Lemon wedges should be cut in the same manner as limes. Often lemons are cut into longer wedges when used for Iced Tea and Bloody Marys.

To cut lemon twists —

1. Cut ½ inch off of both ends of the lemon. Make sure to cut beyond the rind, allowing the meat of the lemon to show.

2. Make one slice, through the skin and rind, down the length of the lemon.

3. Remove the skin only in one piece. If the skin is tough, place the lemon on a hard surface and apply pressure as you roll it. This will soften the skin. Once you remove the skin, trim off any excess white inner rind. This is especially important if the rind is thick.

   Again, the flavor is found in the yellow outer skin - the inner rind can be bitter in flavor.

   – or –

   Using the back, rounded end of a bar spoon, gently work the spoon between the skin and the rind of the lemon, separating the skin from the meat of the lemon until the inside meat can be easily popped out.

4. Cut the skin into strips about ¼ inch wide. If the skin is thick with rind, trim off the excess white portion with a knife.

If you don't have much call for twists, you may peel them off a lemon as needed —

- Cut off the ends of the lemon, exposing the meat.
- Slice lengthwise, through the skin only (stop just before reaching the meat of the lemon).
- Repeat this cut at ¼ inch intervals.
- Peel off fresh twists as required.

To loosen the skins of tough lemons — place the lemon in a bucket of hot water for ten minutes. The skin will be much easier to remove.

The flavor from the twist comes from oils found in the outer skin of the lemon. To release the essence, twist the lemon peel over the drink, run the skin side around the rim of the glass and drop it into the drink.

Many times customers will ask you for a "twist of lime." Most of the time they are referring to a wedge of lime. Make sure to verify what they really want.

FRUIT WHEELS

Lemon, limes, and oranges can be decorative when cut into wheels and placed on the rim of the glass.

To make a wheel —

- Cut off ½ inch from each end of the fruit.
- Make a ¼ inch cut down the length of the fruit (this cut allows you to hang the wheel on the rim of a glass).
- Slice the whole fruit, crosswise, into wheels ¼ inch thick.

ORANGES

Orange slices are decorative and add a nice flavor to tropical drinks, Collins, and Sours.

Cut the orange in half, lengthwise; slice off the ends and make uniform slices of about ¼ inch.

OTHER TYPES OF DRINK TRIMMINGS

CELERY: Used as a garnish, most often for Bloody Marys. Celery should be kept moist and chilled.

CHERRIES: Maraschino cherries are used most often. They are usually red and still have their stems. Cherries are used to garnish tropical drinks, Sours, Collins, and the traditional Manhattan.

CHOCOLATE: Shaved chocolate is used to garnish certain coffee drinks including cappuccinos and lattés.

CINNAMON STICKS: Used to flavor and stir many hot drinks, including hot mulled wine.

CUCUMBER: Used to garnish drinks made with Pimm's.

NUTMEG: Sprinkled on some hot drinks and Brandy Alexanders.

OLIVES: Use green pitted olives for martinis. Keep them covered and refrigerated in their own liquid.

ONIONS: Pearl onions are used to differentiate a Martini from a Gibson. Keep them covered and refrigerated in their own liquid.

SALT: Keep a container of salt handy. Use Kosher salt for rimming the glasses of Margaritas, Salty Dogs and other requests.
To salt a glass: Use a lemon or lime wedge to wet the rim of the glass (save it to garnish the drink), or dip the rim of the glass onto a saucer containing lime juice or sweet and sour mix. Twist the wet rim in the salt. Shake off extra salt before icing your glass.
To ice a salted glass: To keep excess salt from contaminating your fresh ice, hold the salted glass over a nearby a sink or barrel as you ice it. Using an ice scoop, drop the ice slowly and carefully into the glass. Avoid hitting the salted rim with the ice. The taste of salt belongs on the rim, not in the drink.

SIMPLE SYRUP: A liquid sugar mixture used in place of granulated sugar. To make your own: mix 4 cups sugar with 2 cups water. Simmer five minutes, cool, bottle, and always keep some handy.

SUGAR: Use a superfine sugar; it dissolves quickly and easily.

MAKING YOUR BAR WORK

TEAMWORK

Teamwork behind the bar is a number one necessity — always do your share of the work.

There is more to the job than making drinks and collecting tips. Common sense should (but doesn't always) dictate the following —

Never leave a juice container empty or without enough left in it to make another drink. Refill it now.

Never put back an empty bottle or one with just a few drops remaining. Pour it off into the drink and replace the bottle immediately.

Whenever you take the last one or notice something is running low, do something about it! Replenish and replace as you go.

When working a busy bar with multiple wells, be a team player. When you refill your juices, fruit, or ice, check the other wells and refill them at the same time.

Teamwork means knowing when to step up and when to step back — don't let your ego get in the way of your pocketbook.
When you work behind a bar with other bartenders, you are sure to find an interesting mix of personalities. Whenever possible, use these different personalities to directly match bartenders with customers.

For example —

When a group of regular customers or friends of one bartender come in, let that bartender wait on them. They will make you and the house more money.

When a group of rowdy customers comes in, find the bartender who is best suited to diplomatically control this type of customers.

When a group of young-looking customers arrives, have the bartender best at checking I.D.'s take charge.

BAR SETUP AND CLOSING

THINK AHEAD WHEN YOU SET UP YOUR BAR —

- Have enough fruit cut for the day/night shift.
- Fill all straw and napkin caddies.
- Check and stock backup juices, liquor, and beer.
- Count, and verify, your cash drawer.
- Always carry your own pens and wine opener.

BE THE BARTENDER THAT YOU'D LIKE TO FOLLOW

Each bartender must do his part in keeping a clean, well-stocked bar. Do your best to make the shift change smooth and complete. Don't leave your mess for the next bartender unless you plan on leaving behind the tips you made while creating it.

There is no better way to begin a shift than by finding it properly stocked: ice bins filled, clean, hot water in the sinks and fresh coffee on the burners.
Good setup is the sign of a good bartender.

Slow down and/or shut off any borderline customers before your shift is over, <u>no matter how well they have been tipping you!</u> Nothing is worse then beginning a shift with a bar full of over-served customers.

COMMUNICATE WITH YOUR RELIEF BARTENDER

Make sure to relate all important information about any customers or situations that may need to be monitored.

Collect on or transfer any open tabs.

Introduce your relief to your customers. This will notify your customers that your shift is through and will help you collect any intended tips. It will also allow your relief to continue any rapport that you've established with your customers.

Keep a log book behind the bar. This is a great way to communicate between shifts.

AT CLOSING TIME —

Follow bar policy regarding the restocking of beer and liquor (some bars restock at closing, some at opening).

- Make sure all bottles are facing forward and wiped clean.
- Run hot water down all draft beer drains.
- Clean all bar surfaces and trash areas.

KEEPING YOUR BAR HAPPY AND HEALTHY

Remove all dirty glasses from the bar and keep them out of customer view.

Never carry glasses, clean or dirty, by placing your fingers inside the glass.

Check glasses for lipstick before you wash them. Even the best washing methods can leave a signature color behind.

If you hand wash your glasses, pre-rinse any blenders or glasses that have any milk, cream, or creamy liquors (e.g., Bailey's) left in them. It takes only a couple drops of milk in your wash water to cloud it up.

Keep the water in your bar sinks fresh, clean, and hot. Use one sink for wash, one for rinse, and a third for rinse and disinfectant.

Periodically clean all glasses behind the bar.

Place, don't throw, broken glasses or empty bottles into garbage cans. Flying glass can injure you, other bartenders or customers.

If smoking is permitted; Empty and wipe ashtrays often (never empty ashtrays into the trash at closing time, in case any smoldering embers remain).

To remove a dirty ashtray from the bar —

Using one hand, place a clean ashtray, upside down, over the dirty one. Pick both ashtrays up together. Empty, clean and replace. Covering ashtrays when you move them, keeps loose ashes from contaminating drinks.

Do not smoke behind the bar, even when the bar is closed — ashes easily fly into ice bins and glasses, creating an unpleasant drink garnish.

Whenever you sneeze, cough, or blow your nose, do it away from your customers. Then rinse and dry your hands before you finish making that drink!

Keep clean bar towels handy and folded neatly.

Here is one way to fold a bar towel so that it is neat and shows no open seams —

Fold the towel in half, then in half again. Roll the towel, beginning with the open seams (this will hide them; your roll will end up at the folded seam).

Your cleanliness and the cleanliness of your bar are a direct reflection of your bartending abilities.

BARTENDING DO'S AND DON'TS

Keep your eyes and ears open. Monitor any situations that could affect the harmony of your bar.

Welcome everyone to your bar with a smile.

Don't anticipate a customer. Always ask each customer what he would like — even your regulars.

Ask if your customer wants another drink when you see an empty glass. Do not remove the empty bottle or glass until the customer is ready to order another drink or leave the bar.

Serve stemware from its stem. This keeps fingerprints off the glass and keeps your hands from warming the champagne or white wine.

Know your basic drinks and garnishes. If you are not sure of the ingredients, ask!

If you make a mistake with a garnish, the drink will most likely have to be remade. This is especially true with a Martini. Olives, onions, and twists leave behind their own signature oils and taste.

When you remove a pour spout from a bottle, replace it onto a bottle of the same liquor. If a pour spout from a bottle of peppermint schnapps ends up in a bottle of vodka, the taste of the whole bottle may be affected.

A bartender becomes privy to many conversations. Do not join into conversations unless invited, and never repeat anything that you hear or see.

Remember names — make customers feel comfortable, but never mention previous visits or companions.

Never offer information regarding your customers — "How long have they been there" or "Who were they with?" Whatever you see or hear from behind the bar should be kept confidential.

Don't ask personal questions or bring up controversial subjects; you may get more than you bargained for.

If customers are alone, offer some conversation. Open the door for them to enter, but respect their decision if they choose to keep to themselves.

Give equal attention to your customers, even when you have friends sitting at the other end of your bar.

Be sure to thank all your customers and invite them back.

Keep good posture behind the bar. Don't lean and don't chew gum while you work.

If you are serving food at your bar, always excuse yourself from conversation when the food arrives.

Leave your personal opinions and comments at home.

ATTITUDE IS EVERYTHING

Bartenders or cocktail servers cannot be effective at their jobs without the full support and positive attitudes of those they work with.

A smile is just as catchy as a frown. Both will be passed on to anyone in its path. Leave your personal problems at home. If you encounter a problem with someone at work, wait until after service, then discuss it in private.

If you can't bring a smile to work and pass it on, maybe it's time to get a desk job!

STREAMLINING SERVICE

There are times when a bartender will need to muster up all of his physical and mental bartending skills and then some, in order to handle what seems a direct assault on his bar by some impatient, thirsty customers.
When this happens, don't lose control — take control.

WORK YOUR WHOLE BAR
When your bar is two-deep with customers, it is easy to get stuck in one place, pumping out drinks to anyone that happens to be in front of you (or within shouting distance). This type of service will not help your tips or the attitudes of customers outside of your earshot. Show your customers that you are in control.

FIND A RHYTHM AND STICK TO IT
You must have a "method to your madness" — one that is fair, constant, easily explained, and visually recognizable to your waiting customers.

Begin at one end of your bar and work toward the other.

Take orders from those directly against the bar, not those waiting behind them.

Move down the bar (like methodically eating an ear of corn, row by row) until you reach its end.

Begin again from your original starting point. Continue to keep this constant direction and rhythm until the bar slows down or until someone, thankfully, gives "last call."

TAKE MORE THAN ONE ORDER AT A TIME
The chances are good, that if you take orders from four customers at a time, at least two of these orders will be similar. This means that you can save steps and time by serving all four with one trip to the beer cooler or one trip to the well.

Taking multiple orders removes some of the problems that a bartender faces trying to keep track of who was next in line. Your tips and sales will reflect your control of what could easily be an out-of-control situation.

USE ALL YOUR RESOURCES — MAKE EVERY MOVE COUNT
As soon as one hand becomes free from pouring, use it to straw or garnish a drink.

Be aware of the cleanliness of your bar, even when it's busy. Don't walk by dirty glasses, empty bottles, or dirty ashtrays without picking them up on your way.

Remember — keep your eyes and ears open!
Even when you're buried under drink orders, you are still responsible for the well-being and harmony of all situations that affect your bar.

WORKING A SERVICE BAR

Bartenders and wait staff must work as a team to provide professional and timely customer service.

A bartender must balance bar and cocktail service. Although service to the wait staff may take a bartender away from tipping bar customers, it is an integral part of the job. Poor service bartending will affect all aspects of service.

VERBAL DRINK ORDERS

It is important to develop and practice a policy on placing and receiving service orders. This should include —

- How wait staff should signal a bartender for service — without interrupting the bartender's present transaction.
- How to call out orders, grouping drinks by mix and alcohol.
- Shortening drink names: Screwdriver = Driver, Margarita = Marg., and so on.
- Ordering drinks that spoil last, i.e., draft beer or hot drinks.

WRITING AND ABBREVIATING DRINK ORDERS

The use of written abbreviations is important when working a bar that uses checks for table service. Abbreviations provide a clearer and faster method of ordering.

WHEN WRITING AN ORDER USING ABBREVIATIONS —

1. Write legibly.

2. State the alcohol or drink name first.

3. Use a dash (–) or slash (/) to separate the alcohol or drink from the mix or type of service.

4. Specify the mix or type of service.

Example: **BR-W** or **V/X** (Brandy and Water or Vodka Rocks)

LIQUOR ABBREVIATIONS

The following lists give some examples of standard abbreviations used in the industry. Exact abbreviations vary among establishments and geographic locations.

Abbreviations used when ordering drinks from the well usually start with the capital letter of the name of the alcohol.

Well Liquor	Abbreviation	Well Liquor	Abbreviation
Bourbon	**B**	Scotch	**S** or **SC**
Brandy	**BR**	Tequila	**TEQ**
Gin	**G**	Rum	**R**
Vodka	**V**	Whiskey	**W** or **WH**

Call brands can be abbreviated by shortening the name.

Mixed drinks are abbreviated by —

- Shortening the name of the drink. Using the initials of the name of the drink.

- Using one or more of the words from the drink's name.

OTHER WRITTEN ABBREVIATIONS

MIXERS	ABBREVIATION	SERVICE	ABBREVIATION
Water	**W**	Rocks	**X**
Coke	**C**	Straight Up	↑
Ginger Ale	**G**	Back	**Bk**
Soda	**S**	Double	**Dbl**
Seven Up	**7**	Dry	**D**
Tonic	**T**	Splash	**Spl**

On many soda guns tonic is represented with a Q.
Other mixers can be abbreviate by shortening their names —
Orange juice = **OJ**, Cranberry = **Cran**, etc.

Separate new orders by drawing a line directly under the previous order.

To repeat an order — draw a line and write **RE**.

CUSTOMER SERVICE

ACKNOWLEDGMENT

Acknowledgment is a bartender's secret weapon.
Perhaps the most important aspect of professional bartending is customer acknowledgment. Proper acknowledgment (or lack of) will set the attitude and mood of your customers.

Always acknowledge your waiting customers, no matter how busy you are.
Make eye contact, nod, smile — let your customers know that you'll be right with them.

Place a napkin in front of new customers as you take their order. This informs other bartenders that they have been acknowledged.

The most common mistake made by a bartender under pressure is to avoid eye contact with waiting customers. Nothing upsets a customer more than feeling ignored, yet nothing is easier to correct.

A simple acknowledgment will keep your customers happy and buy you time while protecting and even increasing your tips.

BAR COMPS

Each bar has a set policy regarding complimentary cocktails. Some allow comps at a bartender's discretion, some require management's approval, while others ignore the benefits of a controlled comp policy.

Comping a drink, under the right circumstances, can be a great advertising tool for a bar. It rewards good customers for their patronage and newcomers for their curiosity, and will smooth over a variety of situations that adversely affect customer satisfaction.

All comp drinks must be recorded — write them down or ring them in!

Never comp a customer the first drink (Again, individual house policy applies first and foremost!). If policy permits and you want to comp a drink for a customer, allow him to purchase the first drink, then offer the next one "on the house." Often times a customer will stop in for only one drink. By offering to comp the second drink, the house makes money on the first drink (number one rule), and your customer can decide to stay or not. Either way, the offer will have the same positive effect.

"On the house" means just that. When you offer or deliver a comp drink to a customer, it is important to inform him that he is drinking on *"the name of the bar or bar owner."*

It is equally as important that bartenders never imply that a drink is "on them" unless they pay for it directly. Bartenders gain respect from all those around them, when they reach into their own pocket to buy a drink for a customer. Only then can you say, "This one's on me," and really mean it.

FRIENDS AND FREEBIES

When given the privilege of house comping, you are expected to use your judgment in determining the appropriate recipients. Complimentary drinks are reserved for those circumstances that will benefit the house, not for friends short of cash and not for anyone who asks for a free drink.

IS THE CUSTOMER ALWAYS RIGHT?

This is the service business. Your job as a professional is to provide the best service possible. You will find yourself dealing with a variety of customers. Most are easily pleased, but some people, despite your best efforts, will never be happy.

The best way to deal with a customer complaint is to apologize for the problem, making sure to maintain eye contact.

Remain sensitive to the problem while offering solutions to rectify the situation.

Follow up and make sure the problem has been taken care of.

Keep your cool and be professional. If you succeed in solving the problem, this person often ends up being your best customer.

When a customer complains about the alcohol content of his drink, if policy permits, top off the drink with a bit more alcohol, no questions asked. Only do this once per customer! A bit more alcohol is a small price to pay for keeping your customer happy, and for making you and your bar look good.

Know when enough is enough. You cannot please everyone. When you have done your best to solve a problem or complaint and your best just isn't good enough, seek management's help. Managers are trained (and paid) to deal with most types of complaints and problems.

The bottom line. Learn to bend within reason. There will always be those who will test and question your strengths and weaknesses. Know your bottom line, stand by your principles, and expect those you work for, and those you work with, to stand behind you.

CASH HANDLING

CASH

Along with keeping track of drinks and your customers' needs, a bartender is responsible for keeping an accurate cash drawer. Make sure that you count your bank (money in your cash drawer) before beginning your shift. If your bank is short or over, notify management immediately.

Money comes packaged from a bank in the following ways —

Pennies	50¢
Nickels	$2
Dimes	$5
Quarters	$10
Dollars	$25
Fives	$100
Tens	$250
Twenties	$500

To avoid costly mistakes, it is important not to allow any interruptions by customers or wait staff while using the register or counting money.

Concentration is a must. A register that is short or over is a direct reflection of your bartending abilities. It can mean that your customer has received improper change, or it can signal to management that drinks are not being rung in properly.

CASH TRANSACTIONS

Use your time between making and delivering drinks wisely. Try to have the round added up when you deliver it to the customer. When you take your customer's money, look at the bill(s), hold it up in front of them, and announce the denomination of the bill(s).

Example: That will be $4.50 out of $10.00. This removes the chance of any difference in opinion regarding the size of the bill(s) you received.

When you open your register, place the bill on the top of the register drawer (front lip). Or, alternatively, place the bill in the register drawer. Leave the clamp that holds the bills up as you make your change; This will remind you of the size bill that you are making change for.

MAKING CHANGE

Train yourself to always "face" your bills. Keep them face up, going in the same direction (the bank will love you).

Always double-count your change, first out of your register, and again when you deliver it to the customer or wait person.

When you place your customer's change on the bar, always place the big bills on the top and leave the small bills on the bottom. Many customers like to leave their money on the bar as they wander around. Try to discourage this practice. When money is missing, you are sure to feel responsible. By placing the ones on top, hiding any larger bills, you lessen temptation for others to walk away with the money. Another way to protect a wandering customer's money is to place a glass or a customer's drink on top of the bills.

"Sleeper" is the term used to refer to change left by mistake on the bar. It is best to let the "sleeper" sleep in the same place for a while. If you cannot find the owner, place a glass or ashtray over the money to protect it. If you believe that your customer has left, place the change somewhere separate from your own tips (in a cup or glass). This will prevent an embarrassing situation, should your customer return for his change.

TIPS

TIPS

You can be certain that if you give bad service it will be reflected in your tips. Most times, your good service will be rewarded by a good gratuity. There are those times, however, when your ego and pocket book can be hurt by an uneducated customer.

To combat the let-down or anger that accompanies "getting stiffed," keep in mind that — for as many people that do not tip — there are those who over-tip and make up the difference. We cannot educate the world on the practice of tipping. All we can do is hope that someday all of the non-tippers will end up working in service positions from hell and see the error of their ways.

When you have given your best service and, regardless, are "stiffed" on a large bill, resist the urge to educate your customers! See your manager. In some cases they may address the problem on a management level by asking your customers if there was a problem with the service. Sometimes a tip is overlooked or presumed included in the bill. Most times you will have to deal with it, get over it, and move on.

Many restaurants have a policy that allows for the addition of a tip when serving large parties or a hosted (open) bar. This practice, although common, should be disclosed to the customer in advance by management.

TIP TALK

Never discuss your tips or lack of. A good bartender does his job well and accepts the bad tips along with the good. Letting others know how much you make can cause resentment from customers and fellow workers that may be working hard but making less (such as wait staff, bar backs, door men and sometimes even managers). It can also result in people tipping you less, once they find out that their tip is not going to make or break your day!

MAKING MORE TIPS

Here are some tips guaranteed to improve your "tokes" without having to remind your customer that "tipping is not a city in China."

Break down the bills when you give back change to make it easier for your customers to tip you! Many bartenders feel that giving back five ones, rather than a five dollar bill is presumptuous, and are uncomfortable doing this. **Don't be**.

Important: This is the service business where tipping, or the lack of it, is a direct reflection of your bartending abilities. You work for tips (unless independently wealthy). When you are doing your job, give your customer the option to tip or not. Most customers expect a bartender to give them change that allows for a tip.

Increase your tips by the way that you return your customers' change.

Place the change on the bar, not in your customers' hands (unless their hand is extended to you).

Put the coins down on the bar first with the bills on top. Placing the coin on top of the bills makes it easy for a customer to pick up the bills and the coin in one motion. By putting the coins on the bar, under the bills, customers must spend more time at the bar picking up the change. This is the time to thank your customer, making sure that you make eye contact.

Most customers, because you are present, will at least leave the change. When you work in a busy bar, this change adds up, increasing your tips (pouring schnapps on the bar before you put the coins down also works, but I don't recommend it !!).

Always say "*Thank you.*"

The extra time spent in contact both verbally and visually with your customer, after returning the change, will increase your tip.

There are customers that always tip and don't require the recognition of that fact. Still, many customers need to have their tip acknowledged by you and will leave a better tip in front of you or when others are watching than they would have left when unattended or unnoticed on the bar.

IS THIS MY TIP?

You'll often hear a bartender mention the "thirty second rule." This refers to the amount of time that you let a customer's tip/change remain on the bar before putting it in your tip cup.

Discerning when and if money left on the bar is designated to be your tip requires using your bar savvy. Bartenders should be sure that money left on the bar is meant for them before they pick it up. Assuming a tip is yours when your customer isn't ready to give it to you can create an embarrassing situation for both you and your customer.

On the other hand, leaving an intended tip on the bar can cost you money. If a customer sitting at your bar leaves you a dollar tip after paying for his drink and you don't pick that tip up before serving him again, chances are good that your uncollected tip may serve as the gratuity for both drinks. Whereas, had you collected that tip before serving your customer again, your chances of receiving another tip increase.

Many customers are not in tune as to what happens to tips at the change of shift. When they leave a tip at the end of their stay, it is usually intended for those that served them.

So, what does a bartender do when his shift is over but his customers and tips still remain at the bar?

Before you leave the bar, tell your customers that your shift is over. Ask if they would like another drink before you leave. Many of them will get the hint.

If a customer has left money on the bar that you think is intended as your tip but you don't want to seem presumptuous, have your relief bartender nicely ask, "Is this a tip for *your name*?"

If all else fails, let your relief bartender know that certain customers have not had the chance to tip you yet. The relief should split the tip with you accordingly and put your share someplace where you can pick it up at a later time.

Give your customers the opportunity to tip you. Never leave the bar without thanking your customers and letting them know that you're leaving!

DECLARING TIPS

The days of bartenders being able to pay rent with their paycheck and banking the cash tips are gone. Most bartenders are making the same, if not less, than they were ten years ago before the 8% tax rule came into the picture.

The Tax Equity and Fiscal Responsibility Act of 1982 established regulations for the reporting of tips received by employees working in the food and beverage industry. This tax rule made employers responsible for seeing that at least 8% of their gross receipts are reported as tipped income by their tipped employees.

It seems that the government along with the IRS has now upped the stakes. In a recent Supreme Court ruling the IRS can now audit employers, check charge tip receipts, then determine the average employee tip percentage. This is not bad enough; They then assume (now legally) that tips received on cash sales fall in at the same percentage.

Since the employer must pay tax on all employee declared tips, they can now be fined and charged the back taxes on the difference not declared. This puts a great burden on the employer. They must now act as "tip police" or risk a costly audit, fines and back taxes, not to mention the added tax liability incurred.

This new ruling will change the way tips are reported and will cost us all. Do your own research on this. There are some exemptions and no one knows how far the IRS will actually go with this.

Avoid any surprise allocations at tax time by declaring your tips as you go. Many businesses compute this figure and allocate for you on a daily or weekly basis. It is best to keep personal records of your tips, tip out, hours, and if possible, your gross sales.

If you are depositing large amounts of cash into your bank account and declaring minimum tips, be aware that an audit will leave you in tax trouble.

If you plan on applying for a loan in the near future, declare all your tips. Banks loan on verifiable income from your tax returns, not on any undeclared tip income.

TABS

Most bar policies require that you ring in or record each transaction as it happens. When you run a tab, comp a drink, or replace a spilled drink, record it before you get busy and forget. This is a much easier practice than explaining to your boss that you really did plan on ringing in that last drink.

Never give anyone reason to question your integrity!

CHARGE CARDS

Most Important: Make sure that all of the numbers of the charge card have been recorded and are correct. If you are dealing with multiple cards or split checks, pay extra attention. Make sure that the charge card matches the right person.

When you present a charge slip, thank your customer again. A good presentation can increase your tip. Keep the charge slip within sight but do not stand over your customers while they sign out. Keeping track of your charges will assure that each charge gets signed, is filled in properly, and does not get lost.

Occasionally, a customer will sign the slip and forget to include a gratuity.

Remember: **It is illegal to add a tip to someone's credit slip.**

RESPONSIBLE SERVICE

RESPONSIBLE SERVICE

A bartender must be aware of and in control of all situations that may affect the harmony of his bar. Communication is the key to avoiding problem situations. If you refuse service to a customer and house policy allows him to remain on the premise, be sure to inform all other servers.

A responsible house policy is one that stands by a server's decision to refuse service.

The impact that alcohol has on each individual varies under different circumstances. Each person's metabolism is different. The impact of alcohol consumption on individuals can be influenced by body weight and size, by lack of sleep or food, by stress, by health problems, or by drugs consumed with alcohol.

A 12-oz. can of beer, 1½ oz. of 80-proof liquor, and a 5-oz. glass of wine all contain the same amount of alcohol.

Drinking on a full stomach will slow down the alcohol absorption process but will not prevent it.

It takes approximately 20 minutes for the alcohol in a standard serving to be absorbed into the blood stream.

Only time will sober a person. It takes approximately one hour to eliminate one serving of alcohol.

Drinking coffee will not sober a person. Taking the time to sit and drink the coffee while your body works off the alcohol is the ticket.

Bartenders need to be aware of the Blood Alcohol Count (BAC) used in their state to determine the point of legal intoxication. In most states is it illegal to serve a customer that is obviously intoxicated. Your responsibility is to prevent customers from becoming intoxicated. It is also your job to sell and serve alcoholic beverages.

Stay alert to your customers. How are they conducting themselves? Is their walking or talking impaired? Draw them into conversation so you can determine any warning signals or noticeable signs of intoxication. Ask other servers the number and type of drinks that the customer in question has consumed.

DEALING WITH INTOXICATED CUSTOMERS

Perhaps the hardest part of a bartender's job is shutting off a customer. This is when the balancing act begins — the time when the bartender goes from being a "best buddy" to "judge and jury". "To serve, or not to serve?"

The decision to terminate service must not be influenced by how much the customer has been tipping you.

A drunk is a drunk, even when this person is your friend or a regular customer.

SLOW 'EM DOWN

It is much easier to slow a customer's drinking down than to shut off an over-served customer.

You hold the bottles and control the service. When a customer begins to cross the line between good customer and bad customer, it is up to you to keep him in the good range.

When multiple rounds are being purchased for groups, always ask each individual if he is ready for another drink before making it. Never place a new drink in front of a customer until he has finished his last one.

Never pressure anyone to drink, no matter what his friends say!!

To slow down service — visit that area of the bar less frequently and don't ask if they are ready for another. This may be enough to keep borderline customers drinking at your pace.

Eventually, you will be called on to explain your lack of attentiveness. Do not challenge a customer's ability to handle alcohol, especially in front of his friends. Make the customer see the benefits of slowing down. Explain that management is very strict with their policy of not over-serving, and monitors bartenders and customers carefully.

Make the management out to be the bad guy; you are only doing your job. Further explain that you want him to be able to stay and enjoy himself. Offer a complimentary soda, coffee, or water between drinks (if management allows).

SHUT 'EM OFF

Once the decision to terminate service has been made, the next step is to inform your customer. Since you have already determined that your customer is too drunk to serve, you can be sure that his sense of logic is also drunk, making your job just a little bit harder.

Here are some methods for shutting customers off —
Be courteous, but firm. Know what you want to say before you approach your customer.

Don't bargain or back down once you have made the decision to terminate service.

Don't embarrass or challenge your customer in front of others; keep it as low-key as possible. Keep the bouncers away unless your customer becomes unreasonable. The presence of someone flexing his muscles may hurt the situation more than help it.

Don't make judgmental statements such as — "You've had enough" or, "You need to go home." Instead, focus on yourself and the problems you will have if you serve him again. Say, "I can't serve you any more. The police are cracking down and management is very strict with us." Explain that you are very sorry and offer to purchase a drink the next time he comes in (if management allows).

If a customer enters your bar already intoxicated, do not serve him. If he/she is a happy drunk, try a light approach. Greet the customer with a smile, then explain your reasons for not being able to serve him. If your customer is demanding and you sense trouble, call management, bring in the bouncers or call the local police.

Suggest or arrange alternative transportation for intoxicated customers. If they are with a group, find a sober friend to drive them home. Call them a cab. If they refuse, offer to help pay. Some cab companies will split the cost of the fare with the bar when an intoxicated customer can't afford to pay.

If, after all your good efforts, your customer refuses your help in providing a safe ride home, it is your responsibility to protect others on the road. Explain to your customer that you have no choice but to call the police, then follow through.

THE A.B.C.'S OF CHECKING I.D.'S

The Alcoholic Beverage Control Agency (A.B.C.) is a state run agency responsible for the enforcement of liquor laws. It's main objective is to educate the public about responsible drinking and regulations and to enforce the legal and responsible dispensing of alcoholic beverages.

It is the legal responsibility of every alcohol server to verify that the purchasers and consumers of alcoholic beverages are at least 21 years of age or the age set by the individual state.

Every bar should have a set policy regarding the checking of I.D.'s. It is advisable to ask for identification from anyone that appears to be under the age of 30. Some bars make it mandatory for everyone to show proof of age.

WHAT IS ACCEPTABLE PROOF OF AGE?

An I.D. must be issued by a *governmental agency* and include all of the following —

- Name
- Date of birth
- A physical description
- A photograph

Examples of acceptable proof of age —

- Driver's license
- State issued I.D. card
- Federal military I.D. card.
- U.S. passport (foreign passport with photo)
- U.S. government immigrant I.D. card
- It must be currently valid (not expired).

Accept only the forms of identification that you are familiar with. Although the above are all acceptable forms of identification, some bars may choose to accept only licenses from their state.

There are I.D. reference books on the market that show, in detail, all state licenses, official identification cards, green cards (which are actually pink), and military I.D.'s. These books are an important resource for all bars. Keep an updated copy at all locations where I.D.'s will be checked.

Many official looking identification cards can be purchased through newspaper and magazine advertisements. If an I.D. does not match the description found in the book, do not accept it. Your local Alcoholic Beverage Control (A.B.C.) office should be able to tell you where to purchase a good I.D. reference book. **Keep informed**!

CHECKING I.D.'S

Never assume anything when it comes to the checking of identification. **Remember**: the ultimate responsibility and fine is yours!!

Make sure that you are familiar with your state driver's license and identification cards.

Use an I.D. reference book for any out of state identification.

Have the person remove the I.D. from their wallet. You must examine the document directly for alterations. Rub your finger over the photo to make sure it's the original. If it is a paper license, hold a flashlight to the back of the document while looking at the front. This will show any white-out or patch jobs.

Do not accept any altered identification.

Check the expiration date. Do not accept any identification that has expired. Chances are good that it has been passed down by an older sibling or friend.

Card anyone who looks under 30.

LOOK CAREFULLY AT THE I.D.

Check the print. Is it computer generated or typed? Many I.D.'s are altered by laminating false information over the original document. If the I.D. seems suspicious, check the corners for an extra plastic layer. Be careful not to damage the document.

Do the math! Check the date of birth. Know the date and year required for someone to be of legal drinking age.

The A.B.C. can now legally send underage decoys to your bar. These visits are unannounced and intended to catch alcohol servers who are not properly checking I.D.'s. The law requires a decoy to show their I.D. when asked. Their I.D.'s are legitimate, clearly showing them to be underage, yet many people fail to calculate the dates, looking instead, for hidden alterations while skipping over the obvious.

Check the photo. Could this be the same person? Photos from an old passport or old license with an extension can be hard to match. Focus on the similarities or differences in the nose and chin areas.

Check the physical description on the I.D. (height, weight, eye and hair color). Make sure they match the person you are looking at. Be prepared for the usual excuses: "I've lost weight, I've grown, I've shrunk, I'm blond, I just dye my roots black," etc.

Check the age on the I.D. Does the person appear to be as old as the I.D. shows?

If, after following these steps, you still have doubts —

Ask questions from the information given on the I.D., such as date of birth, astrological sign (it helps to keep a list of signs and dates nearby), middle name and address.

Have the person sign his name and compare the signatures. Record all signatures in a notebook. If there are any questions by the A.B.C. or other law enforcement officials, you will have proof that the I.D. was checked.

Ask for a second piece of identification with his name on it. A credit card or bank card bearing his name may help to verify that the identification presented is his.

PROTECT YOURSELF AND YOUR ESTABLISHMENT

A person without proper identification or someone holding a fake I.D. can slip by even the best-trained staff. Even when you believe that a doorman or other employee has checked an I.D., follow your intuition and re-card anyone that seems of questionable age.

Here are a couple of common, potentially costly situations to avoid —

Even if you have seen a person drinking in your bar before, do not automatically assume that the I.D. shown is proper until you see it for yourself. This person may have gained initial entry without showing a proper I.D. and is now relying on the fact that you or your doorman recognize him or her and feels no need to check the I.D. again.

Never assume that a person is of legal drinking age because someone says so. Will this person pay your fine if he is wrong? Most people are unaware of the consequences bartenders face for serving minors and will try almost anything in order to gain entrance.

It is important that **every employee** be aware of, and report, any suspicious behavior signaling that a minor may have gained or is attempting to gain illegal entrance.

Remember: serving minors is an offense that can cause a temporary or permanent revocation of an establishment's liquor license, thereby directly affecting all employees.

Watch out for the following —

A person producing an I.D. from a wallet but unable to produce a second verification, even though you clearly see other cards and documents in the wallet.

Monitor any groups of young people milling outside the bar entrance. Watch for the passing of I.D.'s from friends inside the bar.

Look for their friends inside the bar to be clustered together, near the entrance, discussing how to pass I.D.'s to their waiting friends.

Monitor the exit and re-admittance of these individuals. Require them to produce their I.D. each time they re-enter, even if they have been checked or stamped.

If you suspect that an I.D. has been transferred, allowing a minor to gain entrance, ask each person in the group to produce identification again. Watch for anyone in the group that tries to slip away into the crowd. An excuse often used is: "My friend has my I.D. I'll find it and be right back."

If you are directly responsible for the checking of I.D.'s, keep your eyes open. When a group of young people enter the bar, those without proper I.D. will usually head straight to the bathroom or to an area of the bar where they can blend in without being noticed.

OTHER HELPFUL HINTS

BAR CURES

Cure those stubborn hiccups this way —
Suck on a lime. If that doesn't work the first time, sprinkle bitters on another lime and try that.

Here are some helpful hints for settling the stomach —
Sprinkle ½ teaspoon of bitters into 8 ounces of soda water. Drink it all at once. You can add flavor by squeezing in a lime wedge. This is a great cure for indigestion.

Try a shot of blackberry brandy to get rid of the runs and stomach cramps. Blackberry root is a natural remedy for the stomach.

No back-bar should be without a tube of Super Glue. Use this amazing remedy to seal paper cuts before working with lemons and limes.

Liability issues make it a bad idea for you to dispense aspirin or other "over the counter" remedies to customers.

HANGOVER HELPERS

Medically, a hangover is explained as "severe swelling of cranial arteries and irritation of the gastrointestinal tract's lining." In human terms that means a killer headache and an upset stomach.

Hangovers are more easily prevented than cured. The best way to avoid a hangover, apart from not drinking, is to drink slowly, in moderation, and on a full stomach.

Hangovers have many contributing factors, including stress, physical health, and the amount and rate of alcohol consumed. Another major cause of hangovers is the "congeners" (coloring and flavoring agents) present in all alcoholic beverages. Bourbon, brandy, and rum are high in congeners. Play it "hangover safe" by drinking vodka or white wine, both low in congeners.

Although there are no foolproof remedies for the morning-after hangover, here are a few remedies that may take the edge off —

Alcohol acts as a diuretic. Before you go to sleep and when you wake up, replace fluids with plenty of water and fruit juice. Juice contains fructose, which burns the alcohol in your system more quickly.

Vitamin B-complex along with a 1000-mg. dose of vitamin C will help balance your blood count.

Stick to bland foods high in carbohydrates and fructose.

Caffeine may ease your headache but can leave you with the jitters.

The "hair of the dog that bit you" is a mythical saying. Drinking more alcohol will merely prolong the inevitable.

TOASTING AROUND THE WORLD

ARABIC	BESALAMATI
AUSTRIA	PROSIT
BELGIUM	OP UW GEZONHEID
CHINA	WEN LIE
EGYPT	FEE SIHETAK
FINLAND	KIPPIS
FRANCE	A VOTRE SANTE
GERMANY	PROSIT
GREECE	STIN YGIA SOU
HAWAII	KAMAU
HOLLAND	PROOST
HUNGARY	EGESZSEGERE
IRELAND	SLAINTE
ISRAEL	LEHAYIM
ITALY	ALLA YUA SALUTE
JAPAN	KAMPAI
MEXICO	SALUD
NEW ZEALAND	KIA-ORA
PHILIPPINES	MABUHAY
PORTUGAL	A SUA SAUDE
RUSSIA	NA ZDOROVIA
SCOTLAND	SHLANTE
SINGAPORE	YAM SENG
SWEDEN	SKAL
THAILAND	SAWASDI
ZULU	OOOGY WAWA

METRIC CONVERSIONS

DISTILLED SPIRITS

Metric size	U.S. Fluid Ounces	Closest Container
1.75 Liters	59.2 oz.	1/2 Gallon 64 oz.
1.0 Liter	33.8 oz.	Quart 32 oz.
750 Milliliters	25.4 oz.	Fifth 25.6 oz.
200 Milliliters	6.8 oz.	1/2 Pint 8 oz.
50 Milliliters	1.7 oz.	Miniature 1.6 oz.

WINES

Metric Size	U.S. Fluid ounces	Closest Container
3 Liters	101 oz.	Jeroboam 104 oz.
1.5 Liters	50.7 oz.	Magnum 51.2 oz.
1.0 Liter	33.8 oz.	Quart 32 oz.
750 Milliliters	25.4 oz.	Fifth 25.6 oz.
500 Milliliters	16.9 oz.	Pint 16 oz.
375 Milliliters	12.7 oz.	Tenth 12.8 oz.
187 Milliliters	6.3 oz.	Split 6.4 oz.
100 Milliliters	3.4 oz.	Miniature 2 oz.

DRINKS PER BOTTLE

Glass Size	750 ML	Liter	1.75 Liter
1 oz.	25½	33½	59
1-1/8 oz.	22½	30	52½
1-1/4 oz.	20	27	47½
1-3/8 oz.	18½	24½	43
1-1/2 oz.	17	22½	39½

STANDARD BAR MEASUREMENTS

DASH .... 1/32 oz.

TABLESPOON .... 3/8 oz.

TEASPOON (barspoon) .... 1/8 oz.

JIGGER.....1.5 oz.

PONY...........1 oz.

CUP............. 8 oz.

BAR TOOLS

MUDDLER   WINE OPENER   AH-SO   KNIFE

STANDARD SHAKER   MIXING GLASS   BOSTON SHAKER

STRAINER   SPOON   JIGGER   MEASURER

GLOSSARY

BAR TERMS AND DEFINITIONS

APÉRITIF: Comes from the Latin word *aperio*, meaning "to open." An alcoholic drink taken before meals to open or enhance the appetite. Apéritifs include Vermouth, Campari, Dubonnet, Pernod, and Amer Picon, to name a few.

BACK: Any mixer or beer served separately, accompanying a shot or alcohol served neat. Also called Chaser.

BAR BACK: An assistant to the bartender, responsible for keeping the bar stocked, clean, and running smoothly. A great way to learn the bartending profession.

BAR KNIFE: Keep your bar knife sharp for attractive garnishes. A paring knife is best.

BAR SPOON: A long spoon; use either end for stirring drinks.

BAR TOWEL: Keep them handy around the bar. Towels should be clean, damp and rolled neatly.

To roll: fold the towel in half, then in half again. (This will leave two folded edges and two open edges). Begin to roll from an open edge. Roll the towel so that it finishes with a folded edge.

BOTTLE OPENERS: If you do not have a permanent opener installed next to your beer cooler, make sure to have a sturdy, hand-held opener and a back-up nearby.

BREAKAGE: The alcohol bottles emptied during a given period. Keeping track of breakage is one way of monitoring the amount of alcohol poured.

CARD: To check someone's identification card.

CHASER / BACK / ON THE SIDE: The term used when requesting a beverage to follow a hard liquor. A shot may be requested with a beer chaser or soda back.

CLUB SODA: Water that has been filtered, carbonated, and flavored with mineral salts.

COLLINS: A tall, sweet drink made with sweet-and-sour mix and club soda or Seven-Up. The most popular being made with vodka and gin (Tom Collins).

CORDIAL: Also called liqueur. Cordials are made by either infusion or maceration. Infusion mixes the alcohol with fruits, plants, herbs, flowers, juices, and sweeteners. In maceration, the flavoring agents are steeped in brandy or neutral spirits. Cordials are usually sweet, syrupy, and concentrated.

CORKSCREW: Keep your own handy. No bartender should be without one.

CORKSPOON: A tool used to remove broken cork from inside of bottles.

COOLERS: A tall drink made with spirits or wine and mixed with a carbonated beverage (usually Seven-Up or soda water).

CUTTING BOARD: Always use one. Cutting on stainless bar surfaces will leave scratches and a dull knife. In addition to general cleaning, cutting boards should be periodically cleaned with bleach.

DRY: A term used when referring to the type and/or amount of Vermouth used to prepare a drink.

HOSTED BAR: Open bar for a special event. Drinks are included and paid for by the host.

HOUSE: The restaurant or bar that you work for.

FLASH BLEND: Using a blender just long enough to mix ingredients and crush the ice.

FLOAT: Liquor used or "floated" on top of a drink.

GRENADINE: A sweet, red flavoring made from pomegranates.

HIGHBALL: A basic drink containing liquor, served over ice with a carbonated liquid or water.

ICE SCOOP: Keep one in or around your ice well. Always use your scoop. Broken glass in your ice can ruin a good night.

LIQUEUR: See Cordial.

LIQUOR: A distilled alcoholic beverage.

MIST: A drink served over crushed ice.

MUDDLER: A wooden pestle used to mash and mix ingredients.

NEAT: Liquor served without ice.

"ON THE ROCKS": A beverage served over ice, usually in a rocks glass.

ORANGE FLOWER WATER: An orange flavoring agent used for making Ramos Fizzes.

ORGEAT: A sweet, non-alcoholic almond-flavored syrup.

OVER: Alcohol served over ice.

P.C.: A term used when referring to 'pouring-cost' percentage.

POUR SPOUTS: Pour spouts are used to control the speed at which you pour. Use regular size pourers for most liquors. Thick or chilled liquors and juices may require a pourer with a larger spout (called speed pourers).

POUSSE-CAFÉ: A drink made by layering or floating liqueurs of different densities.

SELTZER: Similar to club soda but without the addition of mineral salts.

SHAKER GLASS: Available in different sizes, usually made of metal. Some shakers will fit over bar glasses, others are available with a matching mixing glass.

SHOOTER: A drink intended for quick consumption.

SOUR: A drink made with sour mix. The most popular is the whiskey sour.

SOUR MIX: Also called sweet and sour. A mix combining lemon and/or lime juice with sugar.

SPEED RACK: The rack usually located closest to your ice bin, used to hold your most frequently used bottles.

SPLASH: A small amount of mixer added to a drink.

"STRAIGHT UP": A term originally used for any cocktail prepared in a mixing glass, strained, and served "up" in a chilled cocktail glass. The terms "up," "straight up," or "neat," may also be used by customers when requesting any drink without ice.

STRAINER: Used along with a mixing glass for straining ice away from chilled shots or cocktails served "'straight up."

STRAWS: Use a straw with all mixed drinks containing ice and with drinks served over ice that contain more than one liquor. Use no straw for a single liquor served over ice or for drinks served without ice.

TODDY: A mixture of a spirit, hot water, and a sweetener served with a lemon twist or wedge. The most popular is made with brandy, sugar, and hot water.

WELL: Alcohol brands poured by the house when no specific brand name is called for. The "well area" is considered the area around the ice bin and speed rack.

WORCESTERSHIRE SAUCE: A sauce originated in England composed of soy, vinegar, anchovies, and spices. Used primarily in Bloody Marys.

RECIPES

ALABAMA SLAMMER

1 oz. Southern Comfort
½ oz. Amaretto
½ oz. Sloe Gin
Orange juice

Highball/Rocks/Bucket glass
Serve over ice *or*
Shake with ice, strain &
Serve up

VARIATION: Substitute Grenadine for Sloe Gin

ANGEL'S TIP

1¼ oz. Dark Crème
   de Caçao
¼ oz. half & half

Cordial glass
Serve up
Float cream on top

APPLETINI

1¼ oz. Vodka
½ oz. Apple Schnapps
or Sour Apple
option - add ¼ oz. Midori

Cocktail glass
Shake or stir
Serve up
Garnish: cherry or orange

B-52

1/3 Kahlúa
1/3 Irish Cream
1/3 Grand Marnier

Cordial/Rocks glass
Serve up
Layer in order listed

BACARDI COCKTAIL

Bacardi Rum
Sweet & sour mix
¼ oz. Grenadine

Champagne/Cocktail glass
Serve up
Flash blend & strain *or*
Shake with ice & strain

BANSHEE

1 oz. Crème de Banana
½ oz. W. Crème de Caçao
Half & half

Champagne/Cocktail glass
Serve up
Flash blend & strain *or*
Shake with ice & strain

BAY BREEZE

Vodka
Cranberry juice
Pineapple juice

Highball/Bucket glass
Serve over ice
Equal parts: cranberry and
pineapple juice

BEAUTIFUL
1/2 Courvoisier or Hennessy
1/2 Grand Marnier

Preheat *Brandy snifter*
Serve up

BLACK RUSSIAN
1 oz. Vodka
½ oz. Kahlúa

Rocks glass
Serve over ice

BLOODY MARY
1 oz. Vodka
Tomato juice
¼ oz. Worcestershire
sauce, fresh lime juice
dash Tabasco sauce,
salt, pepper, celery salt,
horseradish.

Collins/Specialty glass
Serve over ice
Mix well *or* shake
Garnish: celery stalk,
lemon/lime wedge, olive

BOCCE BALL
Amaretto
Orange juice

Highball/Bucket glass
Serve over ice

BOILERMAKER
Bourbon *or*
  Blended Whiskey
Beer chaser

Shot glass
Serve with a beer to chase
down the shot

BRANDY ALEXANDER
¾ oz. Brandy
¾ oz. D. Crème de Caçao
2 oz. half & half

Champagne/Cocktail glass
Serve up
Flash blend & strain *or*
Shake with ice & strain

BRAVE BULL
1 oz. Tequila
½ oz. Kahlúa

Rocks glass
Serve over ice

CAPE COD
Vodka
Cranberry juice

Highball/Bucket glass
Serve over ice
Garnish: lime wedge

CHIP SHOT
1/2. Tuaca
1/2 Irish Cream
3 oz. hot coffee

Rocks /Coffee glass/Mug
Serve up or as coffee drink
Preheat glass

CHOCOLATINI / CHOCOLATE MARTINI
1¼ oz. Vodka
½ oz. Godiva Choc. Liquor
option - use Vanilla Vodka

Cocktail glass
Shake with ice & strain
Garnish: choc.shavings

VARIATIONS: Substitute Crème de Cacao for Godiva, use light or dark Godiva or Cacao, add a splash of Kahlua, use vanilla vodka, rim the glass with chocolate.

COLORADO BULLDOG
¾ oz. Vodka
¾ oz. Kahlúa
Half & half
Splash Coke

Collins/Bucket glass
Serve over ice
Splash Coke on top

COSMOPOLITAN
1¼ oz. Vodka
¼ oz. Triple Sec
¼ oz. lime juice
1 oz. cranberry juice

Cocktail glass
Shake with ice & strain
Garnish: lime wedge

CREAMESICLE
¾ oz. Triple Sec
¾ oz. White Crème
    de Caçao
Half & half

Collins/Specialty glass
Shake & serve over ice

CUBA LIBRE
Rum
Coke
Lime wedge

Highball/Bucket glass
Serve over ice
Garnish: lime wedge

DAIQUIRI
Light Rum
Sweet & sour mix

Collins/Specialty glass
Serve blended
Garnish: lime wheel

DUBONNET COCKTAIL
1 oz. Dubonnet
½ oz. Gin

Cocktail glass
Stir with ice, strain &
Serve up
Garnish: lemon twist

FRENCH MARGARITA
1 oz. Gold Tequila
¼ oz. Cointreau
2 oz. sweet & sour mix
1 oz. lime juice
¼ oz. Grand Marnier

Cocktail/Specialty glass
Serve over ice,
Blended *or*
Shake with ice & strain
Salt glass rim (optional)
Float Grand Marnier on top
Garnish: lime wheel

FUZZY NAVEL
Peach Schnapps
Orange juice

Highball/Bucket glass
Serve over ice

GIBSON
Gin
Dash Dry Vermouth

Cocktail/Rocks glass
Stir with ice, strain &
Serve up *or*
Serve over ice
Garnish: onion

GIMLET, VODKA or GIN
1¼ oz. Vodka or Gin
½ oz. lime juice

A traditional Gimlet is made with
Gin. Verify with customer

Cocktail/Rocks glass
Stir with ice, strain &
Serve up *or*
Serve over ice
Garnish: lime wedge

GODFATHER
1 oz. Scotch
½ oz. Amaretto

Rocks glass
Serve over ice

GODMOTHER
1 oz. Vodka
½ oz. Amaretto

Rocks glass
Serve over ice

GOLDEN CADILLAC
1 oz. W. Crème
    de Caçao
½ oz. Galliano Liqueur
2 oz. half & half

Champagne/Cocktail glass
Flash blend & strain *or*
Shake with ice & strain

GRAPE CRUSH
1 oz. Vodka
½ oz. Chambord
1 oz. sweet & sour mix

Rocks glass
Shake with ice, strain &
Serve up

GRASSHOPPER
¾ oz. G. Crème de Menthe
¾ oz. W. Crème de Caçao
2 oz. half & half

Champagne/Cocktail glass
Flash blend & strain *or*
Shake with ice & strain

GREYHOUND
Vodka
Grapefruit juice

Highball/Bucket glass
Serve over ice

HAIRY NAVEL
1 oz. Vodka
½ oz. Peach Schnapps
Orange juice

Highball/Bucket glass
Serve over ice

HARVEY WALLBANGER
1 oz. Vodka
Orange juice
¼ oz. Galliano Liqueur float

Highball/Bucket glass
Serve over ice
Pour vodka & orange juice
Float Galliano on top

HIGHBALL
A drink served in a highball glass that contains:
one liquor and one carbonated mixer *or* water.

HOT APPLE PIE
Tuaca
Hot apple cider

Coffee glass/Mug/preheated
Garnish: cinnamon stick
or whipped cream

HOT BRANDY
Brandy
1 tsp. sugar (optional)
2 oz. hot water

Preheat *Brandy snifter/mug*
Stir ingredients
Garnish: lemon squeeze

HOT TODDY
1½ oz. Bourbon *or*
    Blended Whiskey
1 tsp. sugar (optional)
2 oz. hot water

Preheat *Brandy snifter/mug*
Stir ingredients
Garnish: lemon squeeze

ICE TEA (Long Island)
See: Long Island Ice Tea

INTERNATIONAL STINGER
1¼ oz. Metaxa
¼ oz. W. Crème
    de Menthe

Rocks glass
Serve over ice

IRISH COFFEE
Irish Whisky
1 tsp. sugar (optional)
Hot coffee
Whipped cream

Coffee glass/Mug/preheated
Top with whipped cream

ITALIAN COFFEE
Galliano Liqueur
Hot coffee

Coffee glass/Mug/preheated
Top with whipped cream

JAMAICAN COFFEE
1 oz. Dark Rum
½ oz. Kahlua or Tia Maria
Hot coffee

Coffee glass/Mug/preheated
Top with whipped cream

JOHN COLLINS
Bourbon *or*
   Blended Whiskey
Sweet & sour + club soda
   or
Collins mix

Collins glass
Serve over ice
Garnish: orange slice &
cherry *or* lime wedge

JONESTOWN PUNCH
¾ oz. Southern Comfort
¾ oz. Amaretto
cranberry juice

Highball/Rocks/Bucket glass
Serve over ice *or*
Shake with ice & serve up

KAMAKAZI
1¼ oz. Vodka
¼ oz. Triple Sec
dash lime juice

Cocktail or Rocks glass
Shake with ice, strain &
Serve up
Garnish: lime wedge

KING ALPHONSE
1½ oz. Dk Crème de Caçao
or Kahlúa
Half & half

Cordial glass
Serve up
Float cream on top

KIOKI / KEOKE COFFEE
1 oz. Brandy
½ oz. Kahlúa
Hot coffee

Coffee glass/Mug/preheated
Top with whipped cream

KIR
¼ oz. Crème de Cassis
White wine

Large Wine glass
Serve up or over ice
Garnish: lemon twist

KIR ROYALE
¼ oz. Crème de Cassis
Champagne

Champagne glass
Serve up
Garnish: lemon twist

VARIATION: Substitute Chambord for Cassis

LEG SPREADER
1 oz. Grand Marnier
¼ oz. Courvoisier
2 oz. hot water

Serve in heated snifter

LEMON DROP #1
1¼ oz. Lemon Vodka
½ oz. sweet & sour mix
Option: splash Seven-Up

Cocktail/Rocks glass
Stir with ice, strain &
Serve up

LEMON DROP #2
1½ oz. Lemon Vodka

Cocktail/Shot glass
Stir with ice, strain &
Serve up

When serving a Lemon Drop as a cocktail: Rub rim of cocktail glass with lemon wedge, dip glass rim in sugar.

When served as a shot: Dip lemon wedge in sugar, serve alongside shot. Customer chases shot with sugared lemon wedge.

LONG BEACH ICED TEA
1/4 Gin
1/4 Vodka
1/4 Light Rum
1/4 Triple Sec
Sweet & sour mix
Cranberry juice

Collins/Specialty glass
Serve over ice
Top with equal parts:
Sweet & sour mix and
cranberry juice
Garnish: lemon wedge

LONG ISLAND ICED TEA
1/4 Gin
1/4 Vodka
1/4 Light Rum
1/4 Triple Sec
Coke
Sweet & sour mix

Collins/Specialty glass
Serve over ice
Top liquors with equal parts:
Coke and sweet & sour mix
Garnish: lemon wedge

LYNCHBURG LEMONADE
1 oz. Jack Daniels
½ oz. Triple Sec
1 oz. sweet & sour mix
Fill with Seven-Up

Collins/Specialty glass
Serve over ice
Garnish: lemon wedge

MADRAS

Vodka
Cranberry juice
Orange juice

Highball/Bucket glass
Serve over ice
Equal parts: orange and
cranberry juice

MAI TAI

1 oz. Light Rum
½ oz. Amaretto
½ oz. Triple Sec
Sweet & sour mix
Pineapple juice
Orange juice
Dark Rum float
Option: sub. Orgeat for Amaretto

Collins/Specialty glass
Pour equal parts:
Sweet & sour, pineapple
and orange juice
Shake & serve over ice
Float Dark Rum on top
Garnish: orange slice *or*
pineapple wedge & cherry

MANGOTINI

1¼ oz. Vodka
splash Triple Sec
2 oz. Mango Juice

Cocktail glass
Shake with ice & strain
Garnish: orange slice

MANHATTAN

1¼ oz. Bourbon *or*
    Blended Whiskey
¼ oz. Sweet Vermouth

Cocktail/Rocks glass
Stir with ice, strain &
Serve up *or*
Serve over ice
Garnish: cherry

MANHATTAN, DRY

1¼ oz. Bourbon *or*
    Blended Whiskey
¼ oz. Dry Vermouth

Cocktail/Rocks glass
Stir with ice, strain &
serve up *or*
Serve over ice
Garnish: lemon twist

A dry Manhattan is made with Dry Vermouth, instead of Sweet.

A Manhattan made with Southern Comfort should use Dry Vermouth
(Southern Comfort is already sweet), and garnished with a lemon
twist.

MANHATTAN, PERFECT

1 oz. Bourbon *or*
   Blended Whiskey
¼ oz. Sweet Vermouth
¼ oz. Dry Vermouth

Cocktail/Rocks glass
Stir with ice, strain &
serve up *or*
Serve over ice
Garnish: lemon twist

One way to remember how to garnish a Manhattan is:
Drinks with Sweet Vermouth get a sweet garnish (cherry).
Drinks with Dry Vermouth get a lemon twist.

Wash the mixing glass thoroughly after mixing a Manhattan
Sweet Vermouth contains small droplets of citrus and herb oils that adhere to the glass. Simply rinsing the mixing glass with water will not remove their odor or taste.

MARGARITA

1¼ oz. Tequila
¼ oz. Triple Sec
2 oz. sweet & sour mix
1 oz. lime juice

Cocktail/Specialty glass
Serve blended
Salt glass rim (optional)
Garnish: lime wheel

It's a good idea to ask the customer if they desire a salted glass. When making a Margarita with fruit, do not salt the glass.

MARTINI

Probably the most popular cocktail of all time.
Martinis are made with Gin, contrary to many "new" drinkers who order a Martini expecting Vodka up with no Vermouth. Best to ask before you make the drink. Remember: it's easier to add more Vermouth than to remake the drink.

1¼ oz. Gin
dash Dry Vermouth

Cocktail/Rocks glass
Stir with ice, strain &
Serve up *or*
Serve over ice
Garnish: olive *or* twist

The traditional Martini is garnished with an olive, but, many people prefer a lemon twist. It is always good to ask, once you insert a garnish the oils and flavor mix with the drink. A mistake with garnish will mean re-making the drink. Although experts say shaking a Martini *bruises* the alcohol, many customers enjoy the icy taste of a well shaken (although diluted) Martini.

Keeping your alcohol in the freezer does help chill the drink faster but does not replace mixing or shaking over ice. The dilution from the ice softens the taste.

MARTINI, DIRTY
1½ oz. Gin
dash Dry Vermouth
dash olive juice

Same preparation as Martini

MARTINI, DRY
1½ oz. Gin
two drops Dry Vermouth

Same preparation as Martini

MARTINI, EXTRA DRY
1½ oz. Gin
1 drop Dry Vermouth

Same preparation as Martini

MARTINI, PERFECT
1½ oz. Gin
dash Dry Vermouth
dash Sweet Vermouth

Same preparation as Martini

MEDITERRANEAN STINGER
1¼ oz. Metaxa
¼ oz Galliano Liqueur

Cocktail/Rocks glass
Shake with ice, strain &
Serve up *or*
Shake & serve over ice

MELON BALL
1 oz. Vodka
½ oz. Melon Liquor
Orange juice

Highball/Rocks glass
Serve over ice *or*
Shake with ice & strain

MEXICAN COFFEE
1 oz. Kahlúa
½ oz. Tequila
Hot coffee

Coffee glass/Mug/preheated
Garnish: whipped cream

MIMOSA
Champagne
1 oz. orange juice

Champagne glass
Garnish: orange slice

MIND ERASER

½ oz. Kahlúa
1 oz. Vodka
Club soda

Highball/Bucket glass
Serve over ice
Pour in order listed
Do not mix

Drink all at once, through a wide straw placed at the bottom of the drink.

MINT JULIP

1½ oz. Bourbon
4 mint sprigs
2 tsp. sugar
1 oz. club soda

Collins glass
Muddle mint, sugar & soda
Add crushed ice
Pour Bourbon, stir
Garnish: mint sprig

MOJITO

1½ oz. Light Rum
6 mint leaves
1½ tsp. Sugar
or simple syrup
1 oz. fresh lime juice
2 oz. club soda

Collins/Specialty glass
Muddle mint, sugar, lime juice
Add crushed ice & Rum
Stir, top with club soda
Garnish: lime wedge, mint sprig

MUD SLIDE

1/3 Kahlúa
1/3 Irish Cream
1/3 Vodka

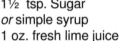

Shot/Cordial/Rocks glass
Serve up *or* blended
Layer in order listed

NEGRONI

1 oz. Campari
½ oz. Gin
½ oz. Sweet Vermouth

Cocktail glass
Stir over ice, strain &
Serve up
Garnish: lemon twist

NUTTY IRISHMAN

1 oz. Irish Cream
½ oz. Frangelico

Rocks glass/Coffee glass
Serve over ice

OLD FASHIONED

1½ oz. Bourbon *or*
   Blended Whiskey
1 tsp. sugar
dash Bitters
1 oz. club soda

Rocks glass
Muddle sugar, cherry, bitters,
orange slice
Pour Whiskey, soda water
Garnish: cherry

ORANGE CRUSH

1¼ oz. Vodka
1 oz. orange juice
splash Seven-Up

Rocks glass
Serve with ice, strain &
  Serve up

ORGASM

1/3 Kahlúa
1/3 Amaretto
1/3 Irish Cream

Rocks/Specialty glass
Serve over ice *or*
Add milk and blend

SCREAMING ORGASM add Vodka

PEARL HARBOR

1 oz. Vodka
½ oz. Melon Liquor
Pineapple juice

Highball/Bucket glass
Serve over ice

PICON PUNCH

1 oz. Amer Picon
¼ oz. Grenadine
Club soda
¼ oz. Brandy float

Collins/Large Wine glass
Pour Amer Picon and
Grenadine into iced glass

Garnish: lemon twist

PIMM'S CUP

1½ oz. Pimm's Cup
Seven-Up

Highball glass
Serve over ice
Garnish: cucumber slice

PINA COLADA
1½ oz. Rum
3 oz. pineapple juice
3 oz. coconut cream
splash sweet & sour
Option: Top with Whipped Cream

Specialty glass
Blend
Garnish: pineapple wedge
and cherry

PLANTERS PUNCH
1½ oz. Myers's Rum
¼ oz. Grenadine
Orange juice
Pineapple juice
151 Rum float

Specialty glass
Serve over ice
Equal parts: orange and
pineapple juices
Float 151 Rum on top
Garnish: cherry & orange

PRESBYTERIAN (PRESS)
Bourbon *or*
    Blended Whiskey
Seven-Up & club soda *or*
Ginger ale & club soda

Highball/Bucket glass
Serve over ice
Equal parts soda
Garnish: lemon twist

PURPLE HOOTER
1 oz. Vodka
½ oz. Chambord
1 oz. sweet & sour mix

Rocks glass
Shake with ice, strain &
Serve up

RAMOS FIZZ
1½ oz. Gin
2 oz. sweet & sour mix
1 oz. orange juice
1 oz. half & half
1 tsp. sugar
1 egg white
dash Orange Flower Water
splash club soda

Specialty glass
Flash blend
Strain & serve up
Top with club soda

RED-HEADED SLUT
¾ oz. Jagermeister
¼ oz. ¼ oz.Peach Schnapps
1 oz. cranberry juice

Rocks glass
Shake with ice, strain &
Serve up

ROASTED TOASTED ALMOND

½ oz. Kahlúa
½ oz. Amaretto
½ oz. Vodka
Half & half

Collins/Bucket glass
Serve over ice
Pour liquors
Fill with half & half

ROB ROY

1¼ oz. Scotch
¼ oz. Sweet Vermouth

Cocktail/Rocks glass
Stir with ice, strain &
serve up *or*
Serve over ice
Garnish: cherry

ROB ROY, DRY

1¼ oz. Scotch
¼ oz. Dry Vermouth

Cocktail/Rocks glass
Stir with ice, strain &
serve up *or*
Serve over ice
Garnish: twist

ROB ROY, PERFECT

1 oz. Scotch
¼ oz. Dry Vermouth
¼ oz. Sweet Vermouth

Cocktail/Rocks glass
Stir with ice, strain &
serve up *or*
Serve over ice
Garnish: twist or cherry

ROOTBEER FLOAT

1 oz. Galliano Liqueur
½ oz. Kahlúa
2 oz. half & half
Coke float

Collins/Specialty glass
Serve over ice
Top with Coke

ROY ROGERS

½ oz. Grenadine
Coke

Collins/Bucket glass
Serve over ice
Garnish: cherry

RUM RUNNER

½ oz. Light Rum
½ oz. Dark Rum
¼ oz. Blackberry Brandy
¼ oz. Crème de Banana
½ oz. Grenadine
Orange juice
Pineapple juice

Specialty glass
Blend with equal parts:
orange & pineapple juice
Garnish: pineapple wedge

RUSTY NAIL

1 oz. Scotch
½ oz. Drambuie

Rocks glass
Serve over ice

RUSSIAN OUAALUDE

¼ oz. Vodka
¼ oz. Bailey's
¼ oz. Kahlua
¼ oz. Frangelico
optional top with cream

Rocks/Highball glass
Serve over ice

There are many variations of this recipe.

SALTY DOG

Vodka
Grapefruit juice

Highball/Bucket glass
Salt glass rim
Serve over ice

SAZERAC

1¼ oz. Bourbon *or*
    Blended Whiskey
¼ oz. Pernod
dash Bitters
1 oz. water
½ tsp sugar

Swirl a few drops of Pernod
into chilled *Cocktail glass*.
Shake with ice, strain &
Serve up

SCARLET O'HARA
Southern Comfort
Cranberry juice

Highball/Bucket glass
Serve over ice
Garnish: lime wedge

SCREWDRIVER
Vodka
Orange juice

Highball/Bucket glass
Serve over ice

SEA BREEZE
Vodka
Cranberry juice
Grapefruit juice

Highball/Bucket glass
Serve over ice
Equal parts: cranberry and
grapefruit juices

SEPARATOR
1 oz. Brandy
½ oz. Kahlúa
Half & half

Collins/Rocks/Bucket glass
Serve over ice
Fill with half & half

SEVEN & SEVEN
Seagram's 7
Seven-Up

Highball/Bucket glass
Serve over ice

SEX ON THE BEACH
1 oz. Vodka
½ oz. Peach Schnapps
Orange juice
Cranberry juice

Highball/Bucket glass
Serve over ice
Equal parts: orange and
cranberry juices

SHIRLEY TEMPLE
½ oz. Grenadine
Seven-Up

Collins/Bucket glass
Serve over ice
Garnish: cherry

SICILIAN KISS
1 oz. Southern Comfort
½ oz. Amaretto

Rocks glass
Serve over ice

SIDE CAR
1 oz. Brandy
½ oz. Triple Sec
1 oz. sweet & sour mix

Cocktail glass
Shake with ice, strain &
Serve up

SILVER BULLET
1 oz. Vodka
½ oz. Peppermint Schnapps

Rocks glass
Serve over ice

There are many variations of this drink. Ask your customer
how they want it prepared before you pour.

SINGAPORE SLING
1¼ oz. Gin
¼ oz. Grenadine
1 oz. sweet & sour mix
Club soda
¼ oz. Cherry Brandy

Collins/Specialty glass
Shake & strain over ice
Fill with club soda
Float cherry brandy on top
Garnish: orange & cherry

SKIP AND GO NAKED
1 oz. Gin
1 oz. sweet & sour mix
Beer

Collins glass
Serve over ice
Fill with beer

SLIPPERY NIPPLE
1 oz. Sambuca
½ oz. Irish Cream
1 drop Grenadine

Shot glass
Layer in order listed
Pour Grenadine into center
of drink

SLOE COMFORTABLE SCREW
1 oz. Sloe Gin
½ oz. Southern Comfort
Orange juice

Highball/Bucket glass
Serve over ice

SLOE COMFORTABLE SCREW AGAINST THE WALL
Follow recipe for Sloe Comfortable Screw.
Float with Galliano

SLOE GIN FIZZ

1¼ oz. Sloe Gin
2 oz sweet & sour mix
Club soda

Chilled Stem glass
Shake with ice *or*
Flash blend Sloe Gin and
sweet & sour mix
Strain into chilled glass
Top with club soda

SMITH & KERNS

1½ oz. Kahlúa
1½ oz. half & half
Club soda

Collins/Bucket/Specialty
Serve over ice
Top with club soda

SNAKE BITE

1¼ oz. Yukon Jack
¼ oz. lime juice

Rocks glass
Serve over ice

SNOWSHOE

1 oz. Wild Turkey
½ oz. Peppermint Schnapps

Rocks glass
Serve over ice

SNUGGLER

Peppermint Schnapps
Hot chocolate

Coffee glass/Mug/preheated
Top with whipped cream

SOMBRERO/Kahlúa & cream

Kahlúa
Half & half

Highball/Rocks/Bucket glass
Serve over ice

SPANISH COFFEE

1 oz. Brandy
½ oz. Tia Maria
Hot coffee

Coffee glass/Mug/preheated
Top with whipped cream

SPRITZER

2/3 White Wine
1/3 club soda

Collins/Large Wine glass
Serve over ice
Garnish: lemon twist

STINGER
1¼ oz. Brandy
¼ oz W. Crème de Menthe

Rocks glass
Serve over ice

SUMMER BREEZE
Vodka
Lemonade
Cranberry juice

Highball/Bucket glass
Serve over ice
Equal parts: lemonade and
cranberry juice
Garnish: lemon wedge

TEQUILA POPPER (Slammer)
1¼ oz. Tequila
1 oz Seven-Up

Rocks glass
Serve up

Place napkin over glass. Firmly cover glass with palm of hand.
Tap bottom of glass on bar to foam. Drink immediately.
Follow with lime wedge

TEQUILA SUNRISE
1¼ oz. Tequila
¼ oz. Grenadine
Orange juice

Highball/Bucket glass
Serve over ice
For sunrise effect, pour
juice last.

TOASTED ALMOND
¾ oz. Kahlúa
¾ oz. Amaretto
Half & half
Amaretto.

Collins/Highball/Bucket glass
Serve over ice
Equal parts: Kahlúa and

TOM COLLINS
Gin
Sweet & sour + club soda
       or
Collins mix

Collins glass
Serve over ice
Garnish: orange slice &
cherry *or* lime wedge

VENETIAN COFFEE

Brandy
Hot coffee

Coffee glass/mug/preheated
Top with whipped cream

VIRGIN MARY

See Bloody Mary recipe, omit Vodka

VODKA COLLINS

Vodka
Sweet & sour + club soda
or
Collins mix

Collins glass
Serve over ice
Garnish: orange slice &
cherry *or* lime wedge

VODKA GIMLET

See Gimlet, Vodka, Gin

WASHINGTON APPLE

1/3 Crown Royal
1/3 Apple Puckers
1/3 cranberry juice

Rocks glass
Shake with ice, strain &
Serve up

WATERMELON

¾ oz. Southern Comfort
¾ oz. Amaretto
½ oz. orange juice
½ oz. pineapple juice
dash Grenadine

Rocks glass
Shake with ice, strain &
Serve up

WHISKY SOUR

1½ oz. Bourbon *or*
    Blended Whiskey
2½ oz. sweet & sour mix

Specialty/Rocks glass
Shake with ice *or*
Flash blend
Strain & serve up

WHITE RUSSIAN

1 oz. Vodka
½ oz. Kahlúa
Half & half

Rocks/Highball/Bucket glass
Serve over ice

*May be made in a highball glass using more half & half.

WINE COOLER

2/3 Red *or* White wine
1/3 Seven-Up
splash orange juice
    (optional)

Collins/Large Wine glass
Serve over ice
Garnish: lemon twist

WINE SPRITZER

2/3 White wine
1/3 Soda water
splash orange juice
    (optional)

Collins/Large Wine glass
Serve over ice
Garnish: lemon twist

WOO WOO

1 oz. Vodka
½ oz. Peach Schnapps
1 oz. cranberry juice

Rocks/Highball glass
Shake with ice, strain &
serve up *or* serve over ice
(add more cranberry juice)

ZOMBIE

1 oz. Light Rum
½ oz. Dark Rum
½ oz. sweet & sour mix
1 oz. orange juice
1 oz. pineapple juice
½ oz. Grenadine
float 151 Rum

Collins/Specialty glass
Shake ingredients with ice
Pour into glass
Top with ice to fill glass
Float 151 Rum on top
Garnish: orange slice &
cherry

~ Recipe Notes ~

~ Recipe Notes ~

~ Recipe Notes ~

~ Recipe Notes ~

～ Recipe Notes ～

INDEX

~Notes ~

~Notes ~

~Notes ~

~Notes ~

~Notes ~

~Notes ~

~Notes ~

ABOUT THE AUTHOR

Lori Marcus has created a successful mix, combining over two decades of bartending experience with a personal style admired and appreciated by customers and co-workers from coast to coast.

Throughout the years, Lori became well known for her strong mechanical bartending skills. After taking a break to open and operate a successful restaurant in Vermont, she moved west to Lake Tahoe and back to the bartending profession.

Returning behind the bar brought the realization that strong physical skills were no longer enough. With changing laws, products and attitudes, today's bartender must be versed in all areas of the profession. *Bartending Inside-Out* is the result of her extensive research and provides the knowledge necessary to reach this professional level of service.